# Sad Love

# Sad Love

## Romance and the Search for Meaning

## Carrie Jenkins

polity

First published in 2022 by Polity Press

Polity Press
65 Bridge Street
Cambridge CB2 1UR, UK

Polity Press
101 Station Landing
Suite 300
Medford, MA 02155, USA

ISBN-13: 978-1-5095-3958-1
ISBN-13: 978-1-5095-3959-8 (pb)

A catalogue record for this book is available from the British Library.

Library of Congress Control Number: 2021951320

Typeset in 11 on 14 pt Fournier by
Cheshire Typesetting Ltd, Cuddington, Cheshire
Printed and bound in Great Britain by TJ Books Limited

The publisher has used its best endeavours to ensure that the URLs for external
websites referred to in this book are correct and active at the time of going to
press. However, the publisher has no responsibility for the websites and can make
no guarantee that a site will remain live or that the content is or will remain
appropriate.

Every effort has been made to trace all copyright holders, but if any have been
overlooked the publisher will be pleased to include any necessary credits in any
subsequent reprint or edition.

For further information on Polity, visit our website: politybooks.com

# Contents

# Preface

When I set out to write a book about love in 2017, I was not happy. I was pretty sad. But I was still in love, or at least so I thought. All the messages from the culture around me were telling me what they had always told me: that being in love was about being happy. Being happy ever after. Happy *with* someone. Happy together.

I had some questions. What if I'm not happy? What if I'm sad – or worse, depressed? Does that mean I'm no longer in love? Am I now unloving? Unlovable?

I desperately hoped the answer to the last two was "no." And I strongly suspected that *was* the answer. Even though I wasn't happy, and didn't know when, how, or even whether I would become happy in the future, I didn't seriously doubt that I was in love with my partners. So instead, like any good logician, I questioned the other assumption: the one about how being in love means being happy.

Being a philosopher by tendency, as well as by academic training, I wanted to think this assumption through, so that I could talk back to it (in my own head, first of all) with some confidence and conviction. Why had I been associating romantic love with happiness? What is the point of that association? Where does it come from? What are its effects?

Of course we all know that "happy ever after" comes from fairy tales, and we know fairy tales for what they are: fictions and fantasies.[1] Real love isn't always happy. I knew that. But a fantasy is powerful, even when we know what it is. Our fantasies – our *ideals* – have a crucial part to play in shaping our lives. An ideal is something to strive for, something we can measure ourselves against and find ourselves wanting.

Maybe I was still in love, but I was inclined to feel as if my sadness was a kind of *failure* condition for my relationships. Good love – ideal love – should be happy ever after, shouldn't it? To say that the romantic "happy ever after" is unrealistic does nothing to diminish its status as an ideal, and hence its power to convince us we are falling short.

The way I think things through is by writing, so in 2017 I started writing this book. But, as I wrote, the world turned, and it is now a very different place compared to how it was when I started. This book goes to press in 2022, in the echo of authoritarian challenges to democracy in the world's most powerful nation, after years of watching the COVID pandemic hammer away at everything from the global economy to our intimate relationships. It took me a lot longer to write this book than I had originally planned. And it exploded into something bigger than what it was originally supposed to be.

*Sad Love* turned out to be more than a theory of romance. It's become a recipe for living in the world as it is now. To be sad, even heartbroken, does *not* mean one cannot love – one's partner, one's country, or even humanity. But to appreciate what love is under circumstances such as these, I needed a very different understanding of love from the one I had been taught. One that diverges radically from the stories and the stereotypes. Love that comes with no promise, and perhaps even no *hope*, of a "happy ever after," but is not lessened or degraded by that. Love whose aim, and whose nature, is something other than happiness.

That changes everything.

But, before I get to that, let me take a step back. What did I have to be so sad about in 2017? That was when my first book[2] on the philosophy of love came out. I did a lot of interviews. I mean a *lot* of interviews.[3] People like to talk about love, I guess. Certainly there aren't enough opportunities to talk about love – at least, not in public. I don't mean opportunities to exchange clichés – there are plenty of those. I mean *really* talk about love. In my book, I was trying to open some space for all the "weird" questions that everyone has, the ones that we aren't supposed to ask in polite company. So maybe that's part of why I was suddenly in demand.

It's not the whole story, though. What the interviewers really wanted to talk about was not my theories so much as my personal life. In the book, I mentioned having a husband and a boyfriend at the same time (with everyone's knowledge and consent). I described some of the challenges of this – the stigma, the awkwardness, the social pressure – canvassing research as well as my own experiences. I talked a little bit about what life can be like as an openly non-monogamous woman with two partners. (The short version: relentless slut-shaming.)

Still, there are lots of books about the experience of being non-monogamous. What made mine worth an interview? Here's one guess: it had something to do with who I am. There's the fact that I'm a woman, of course, which might make me a more interesting spokesperson for non-monogamy than a man would be: we are, after all, strongly conditioned to think of monogamy as something women want and men get pressured into. But there are also quite a lot of books about non-monogamy written by women. (Because there are quite a lot of non-monogamous women.) There's the fact that I am a professor at a university, and maybe people took that to mean that I had thought about these things or that I'd done my homework. That might have been part of it.

But, more than that, I think it was just that I'm a professional, middle-class, middle-aged white woman. I look "normal" and . . . well, *respectable*. I don't look like a rebel, a rule-breaker, a defier of social norms. I look average. Kind of boring. Paradoxically, I think that's why I was interesting.

Polyamory is a form of consensual non-monogamy. Non-monogamy because it involves being open to more than one loving partner/relationship and consensual because it's intentionally chosen by all parties involved (as opposed to cheating, which is non-consensual non-monogamy).

I remember a profile piece in the *Chronicle of Higher Education*. It was written by Moira Weigel, a journalist and author I admire. She came to meet me in Vancouver while researching the piece and we chatted on my front porch, went for sushi, then chatted some more. She wrote a strong profile, a little snapshot of me at a moment in time. When I read it, I saw my own reflection in her mind, an image both familiar and strange. A woman who smoked on her patio and wouldn't talk about one particular topic. Whose dog still smelled of tomato juice after a close encounter with a skunk.

When it was decided that it would be the cover story for the *Chronicle Review*, the journal sent a photographer to my house to shoot me together with both of my then partners. Now, I am not a natural in front of a camera. Being looked at makes me awkward and self-conscious. It's not just that I'm nervous about my appearance (although I am), there's a moral component. Even a passing glance from a stranger makes me feel judged.

The house I lived in at the time was also not easy for a photographer to work with. It was small and dark. Built in the Edwardian era, houses like this are a rarity in Vancouver, but they can make a British export like myself feel homey and nostalgic. Eventually the *Chronicle*'s photographer settled on the best (or least worst) option – upstairs in the room I used for writing, where there's a bit of natural light from the window. The photographer posed me by the window, in my writing chair, with my partners standing behind me. Then, to get the best angle, he crouched back inside of a cupboard full of my clothes.

I was intensely aware of my partners' bodies, peripherally visible to me as I sat in my chair. Both of my partners, in their different ways, seemed so comfortable with being photographed. With being seen. One of Jonathan's many talents is stage performance – he is an amateur operatic singer with a gorgeous, rich, warm baritone voice that I love hearing around our house. Ray has years of experience in front of a camera, and anyway their entire being constantly radiates a fierce, model-like grace, even when they're just walking round Save On Foods.

In the photo, we look like a rag-tag team of superheroes. I love it. Ray and I are no longer partners, and so this image has come to bear even more weight, capturing as it does a phase in my experience of love that I once hoped would be permanent but feels strange and distant to me just a few years on.

And then there it was on the cover of the *Chronicle Review*, emblazoned with the headline: "Can Carrie Jenkins make polyamory respectable?" You know, no pressure.

*Respectable*. It's such a double-edged word. Was I actually trying to make polyamory respectable? Did I even want that? I would love for polyamory and other "weird" relationship forms to be deemed worthy of respect, the way "normal" relationships are. But do I want them to become bourgeois, stuffy, conventional?

There's an old-established journalistic rule that says: if the headline is a question, the answer is "no." I think the rule applies here. Nobody does things like that – no individual person. What I am good at is starting conversations and nudging them in under-explored directions. That's how I see my work as a philosopher.

Anyway, back to why I was sad. When *What Love Is and What it Could Be* came out, and I started doing all those interviews, well-meaning friends and colleagues would say, "It must be nice for you, with your book getting all that attention!" But it wasn't nice.

I'm an introvert for one thing. For another, much bigger thing, a lot of the attention was pure hate. Shortly after publication, ABC Nightline made a short news segment on my life and work, broadcast on national US television. They also posted it to their Facebook page. The top comments were "Immoral," "Odd balls," "Fucked up," "Sick," "It's stupid," and "Interesting." (Thank you, whoever you were, for swimming against the tide.)

Some spend more time crafting their responses. "THIS WOMAN IS A DISGUSTING ANIMAL," someone posted on one of my old YouTube videos:

> A far far left-wing freak that desires to completely over-throw Western Christian Civilization. IT'S WAR ON your ethos Carrie! Every God-loving human on this planet needs to realize WE ARE AT WAR with these commies. End of Story. Oh forgot to add: PLEASE CHOKE YOURSELF CARRIE. Thanks and have a nice God-loving, mom, the flag and apple pie. God Bless America. Let Freedom Ring. Stand up and defend your 2nd Amendment rights. Have happy Christ-centered marriages with lost [*sic*] of Christian children who hug and feed the poor and . . .

This continued into several more posts, none of them reassuring.

My mental health took a nose dive. That wasn't all about the book, to be fair. There was a lot going on in the world at the time. Between the time of writing and the little launch in my university's bookstore in February 2017, the most powerful nation in the world had elected Donald Trump as its leader. Hate was on the rise everywhere, or so it seemed.

There's an Islamic *hadith* (saying) that I like: "If the Day of Judgment erupts while you are planting a new tree, carry on and plant it." I tried, I really did. But it was a complicated time to get people talking about the intricacies and subtleties of love.

For me personally, the hate just kept coming. Every time an interview or article appeared in a high-visibility venue, a stream of nasty feedback would follow in its wake. The public eye does not look kindly on women with ideas. (This is not a new phenomenon – women have not historically been welcomed with open arms to the pursuit of wisdom. The internet just offers us new ways of burning and drowning our witches.)

At the time it was a bit of a blur. But, in retrospect, the hate fell into three buckets. First there was a bucket of hate for feminists. One time, my Twitter account was drowned in hate after I wrote an opinion piece for the Spanish newspaper *El País*, the headline of which (possibly the only part many people read) was "Polyamory is a feminist issue." The article was published in Spanish and most of the reactions were, likewise, in Spanish. I don't speak Spanish, but I was surprised at how much I could understand.[4]

The second bucket is for slut-shaming hate. I am a woman who talks publicly about being polyamorous, so I have been called all the derogatory words you can think of for a promiscuous woman. There are no male equivalents for these words. This was predictable, although knowing something's coming and knowing what it will be like are not the same thing.

I simply wasn't ready for the third bucket: the racism. My husband Jonathan is half Asian, my then partner Ray is Asian, and I'm a white woman who has spent most of her life with the privilege of having racism largely hidden from me. "Ray and Jon [*sic*] look like brothers . . .," declared one anonymous email. "Are they both Chinese? I bet they cook you nice spring rolls for breakfast but whose spring rolls are better . . ." One Facebook message – in its entirety – read, "gross! are asians the only men who will f u?"[5]

I know it's tempting, but the solution to this problem doesn't begin with the word "Just . . ." *Just don't read the comments*; *just don't talk about polyamory*; *just remove yourself from Twitter and YouTube and email and the internet and public discourse.* These are not solutions. If I stop talking and stop engaging, the game is up. In any case, these reactions to my work are among my source materials and my clues. They help me understand the social mechanics operative behind the scenes. This is work I care about, and I can't simply look away without giving up on it.

What other strategies are there, then, besides silence? One option is talking more. I started admitting to my poor mental health in some of my talks and public appearances. I talked about how depression makes it harder for me to perform in all kinds of ways that once came easily. At first I intended to be making excuses for my impaired performance, but I found my audiences really appreciated these acknowledgements. It meant something to them that I was making the costs of the work visible.

I started admitting, too, where I had made mistakes in my own work rather than hiding them. That was painful. I felt ashamed. Then I started talking more about feeling ashamed, and the same rush of relief and recognition came back to me. In academic circles we are trained to see our mistakes as failures, and admitting them is regarded as a weakness. (Academia can be a heartless place. Ideas and ideologies can get quite stagnant and rotten in there. I don't think this is a coincidence.)

The other strategy that sometimes works is not doing anything at all. A piece in the *American Spectator*, about me and a few other authors, said that now we feminists "even hate love." It was high-visibility coverage, so it sent my way a lot of readers who would never have heard of me otherwise. Contemporary ideas about love are constantly swirling around me, and just by being here I can alter their course. Even (or perhaps especially) when I'm staying still.

A strategy that *doesn't* work is retreating into academia. The problem with that strategy is that there is no retreat to be found in academy – or anywhere else, for that matter – from the ideas and culture that shape our lives. Academia is made of people, and people bring that baggage along with them wherever they go.

I'm based in an academic philosophy department, and philosophy is (still) a notoriously male-dominated discipline.

Women in philosophy are a challenge to its self-image as hyper-rational, hyper-logical, hyper-scientific – all male-coded qualities. The discipline represents its history as a procession of "great men": Socrates, Plato, Aristotle, Kant, Wittgenstein, Nietzsche. It might be able to accommodate the presence of the occasional woman displaying presumed markers of those male-coded qualities – a loud voice, an aggressive argumentative tone – but she is more tolerated than celebrated. As Samuel Johnson infamously said, "a woman's preaching is like a dog's walking on his hind legs. It is not done well; but you are surprised to find it done at all."

Before I became a philosopher myself, I had pictured philosophy as something more humane. More compassionate and co-operative. Something that belongs everywhere and to everyone, not just to a few experts working within well-defined fiefdoms of prestige. I imagined philosophy as a perpetual conversation, a massive collaboration. But all this is antithetical to the mundane concerns of real academic institutions: concerns about rankings, and grant dollars, and prizes, and esteem indicators. The scholarly dreams of so many would-have-been philosophers are swallowed up by these things. Condemned to death by a thousand administrative paper cuts.

This contemporary model of a university functions like an addiction to video games or social media. Thoughts of "winning" and "status" motivate us to keep playing, keep scrolling, while the life we thought we wanted slips away.[6] Constantly comparing oneself with others easily induces anxiety and paranoia, as we are invited to feel that we aren't measuring up.[7] We're told we cannot step off the treadmill for a moment, or we'll get left behind. It's easy to see how all kinds of problems get swept under the rug by academic institutions eager to hang on to their high-prestige "stars," to keep up appearances, to cling to position.

Looking back, I suppose I was one of Johnson's dogs. I learned to walk on my hind legs, was promoted early, and had a great track record of publications and lots of inter-national conference invitations. I really felt like a "winner" by all the metrics I'd internalized. It felt good to compare myself with other people and be pleased with the contrast. I'm not proud of this.

But it felt nice when I thought retreating into a small corner academia would be possible, and when I was content to rack up esteem indicators and grant funding. These days, when people say it "must be nice" that my work gets atten-tion, I try to explain. Actually it's difficult, and often kind of horrible. But I still think it's worth doing. Trying to do this other kind of work is awkward and uncomfortable. I can't coast on my achievements (such as they are), because they aren't going to get me where I'm going. Not even close. As soon as I started working on love, and trying to communicate my ideas beyond the narrow walls of academic philosophy, I realized I needed all kinds of skills that I didn't get any help with during the course of my ten years of academic training.

Most urgently, I needed to learn other ways of communi-cating. I had learned to write only for the others in my small corner of academia. Scholarly journal style, it turns out, isn't the way to most people's hearts and minds. (Who knew!) So I went back to school. This is not a metaphor. I enrolled in the Creative Writing MFA program at my university. I became a student again, part-time, alongside my day job.

All my academic training had been focused on rigorous argumentation – drawing clear, straight, black and white lines from point to point. Don't get me wrong here: I am grateful for this skill, and it's a privilege to have had the many years of education it took to hone it. It's not only an academic skill that helps me write papers, it's a life skill that helps me survive. But, as with any tool, it is limited, and there are certain kinds of philosophical work it cannot do. And I feel drawn to some of those kinds of work. So I've had to learn more skills, not to *replace* the skills I learned in my first forty years of life but to supplement them.

I've been learning to write and think more like a novelist or a poet or a journalist, or sometimes all three at once. It's not that it's *wrong* to proceed in straight, rigorous argumentative lines. In the same way, there are times when intricate black and white line drawings are the best way to illustrate something: when close technical details are of the essence and anything else would be a distraction. It's just that, if you are trying to paint a whole scene, a complex landscape with diffuse ambient lighting and confusing shadows, you aren't going to depict *that* subject very realistically if straight black and white lines are the only marks you know how to make.

I completed my MFA degree during the COVID pandemic and, along with the rest of the class of 2020, graduated online. But, for the previous few years, I'd been switching out my professor hat for my student hat as I walked between the philosophy corridor and the creative writing corridor.

Doing and being many things at once doesn't feel weird to me. I prefer it to the kind of intensive focus and specialization I was trained to think was normal and appropriate for an academic. My mind works better (and feels more functional) when it can stabilize itself with a broad base.

In the same way, being in more than one relationship at the same time doesn't feel weird to me. In fact, when I am struggling with my mental health, having more loving partners on hand is a good thing. The work of supporting me doesn't all have to fall on one person.

Which brings me back to that sadness I was talking about. It's easy to imagine how some partners might react to their loved one deciding to pursue a line of work that was evidently making them miserable. Easy to imagine concern, or distress, followed by advice to quit and return to the comfortable old life. It's easy to imagine, really, a partner simply not wanting to be with me if I insisted on making myself miserable like this. Isn't love supposed to be all about the happy ever after?

Well, love is "supposed" to be monogamous too, and mine isn't. When I was at my most depressed, not even the love of my partners could make me feel *happy*, but it did help to make me, and my work, feel possible.

Their recognition and support for who I chose to be, and what I chose to do, was an expression of love. Advising me to quit would not have been. Reflecting on that difference – between love that makes me feel happy and love that makes me feel possible – is what set me on the course towards the main conclusion of this book, which is a new theory of love. This new theory doesn't compete with or replace my work in my first book, *What Love Is*, but it tackles a different part of the question. This book is about my theory of sad love. Or, more accurately, my theory of *eudaimonic* love, which has room for the full gamut of human experiences and emotions, positive and negative, happy and sad.

Eudaimonic love means literally "good-spirited" love. It's going to take me a while to explain what the relevant "spirits" are, but along the way I'll be able to explain what eudaimonia does (and doesn't) have to do with romance, and happiness, and finding meaning in life. I have stopped asking the old question I was taught to prioritize – how to be "happy ever after." This question doesn't interest me anymore. It doesn't look significant.

I just ambitiously promised a "new theory." A new theory? Like a great new idea? A work of startling original genius?

The myth of the great idea works in much the same way as the myth of the "great man." In fact, the two mythologies go hand in hand: we imagine our "great men," such as Darwin or Newton, coming up with their "great ideas," such as evolution or gravity, and we imagine them doing it all alone, as if they existed in an intellectual vacuum. We ignore the contributions of other people, especially "inconsequential" people, such as Darwin's hairdresser, who chatted to Darwin about his experience with pedigree dogs.[8] And we ignore the influence of existing ideas, especially ideas we don't consider respectable, such as alchemy and the occult,[9] which fascinated Newton and were hardly irrelevant to his willingness to theorize "unseen forces" at work in the universe.

In reality, great ideas grow, live, and die in, and as parts of, intellectual ecosystems. (So do terrible ideas, of course. And mediocre ideas.) When I promise you a new theory, what I'm promising to do is build you something out of bits and pieces I've found swirling around in my ecosystem. Some of them are very old, and some have only just appeared. I work like a magpie, gathering shiny ideas from my environment. A curator. Most of what I'm gathering is not rocket science (although it is, in some cases, science). But it's what I'm trying to build from it that matters.

I'll have a "new theory" if I find enough shiny pieces to build a mirror, and that mirror shows us something we need to see.

# Acknowledgements

I am immensely grateful to Jonathan Jenkins Ichikawa, Tyler Nicol, Robin Roberts, Kupcha Keitlahmuxin, Mezzo, Drusilla, and Seven, and to all the good daimons in my support network of friends and family.

For conversations, questions, and comments I am indebted to Chase Dority, Alice Maclachlan, Shannon Dea, Alan Richardson, Jasper Heaton, Jelena Markovic, Chelsea Rosenthal, Dominic Alford Duguid, Cat Prueitt, Kim Brownlee, Chris Stephens, Fatima Amijee, Keith Maillard, Ray Clark, Adriana Jones, Marian Churchland, Jessica Lampard, Alyssa Brazeau, Susan Sechrist, and Ray Hsu. Thanks also to audiences at the University of Manitoba, Simon Fraser University, and the Minorities and Philosophy Flash Talks series, who gave me comments on earlier versions of the material.

My patient editor Pascal Porcheron, and two anonymous readers for Polity, gave me substantial feedback that helped me shape the book into this final form.

Parts of the text and/or related materials appear in previously published work:

- "When Love Stinks, Call a Conceptual Plumber," in E. Vintiadis (ed.), *Philosophy by Women: 23 Philosophers Reflect on Philosophy and Its Value* (London: Routledge, 2020).
- "Love isn't about happiness. It's about understanding and inspiration," *New Statesman*, April 2020.
- "How to 'love-craft' your relationships for health and happiness," *The Conversation*, September 2018.

The work was completed on the traditional, unceded territories of the Musqueam, Squamish, and Tsleil-Waututh First Nations.

# Introduction

Tell a philosopher you love her, and you'd better be ready to define your terms.

It's funny because it's true. Well, sort of. Some philosophers spend their entire working lives on questions of definition or the analysis of concepts. And this is not a pathology. It's important. Put a concept such as *love* under the microscope and you see how vague and fuzzy it is. How layered. Where the spiky bits are. Patterns invisible to the naked eye suddenly become fascinating objects of study.

That's why some of us spend our whole lives trying to get a better look. Philosophy, when it's working well, offers us a treasury of intellectual and imaginative tools: new ways of seeing things. Conceptual microscopes, of course, but also conceptual telescopes, and distorting mirrors, and tinted lenses ... we need all kinds of different approaches. We need to examine our concepts close up, but we also need to get a better look at the ones that feel remote, and we need ways to look at things from new angles, through different filters. That includes the things we *think* we understand, the things most familiar to us. In fact, it's especially important to examine those, as they're often highly influential in structuring the way we live (whether or not we appreciate their playing that role). Deflecting and diffracting our most familiar images can reveal something totally new, perhaps something we would never have imagined it was possible to see.

As I suggested in my preface, this particular book is an attempt to build a conceptual mirror. I'm trying to reflect back to us an image of ourselves, and specifically of our

ideas and ideals of romantic love. It's not an entirely flatter-
ing image, the one I end up with. It's almost grotesque. No
doubt there are some distortions. But, as I said, sometimes
we need a new angle, a vantage point from which the familiar looks weird.

I start from a curiosity about the real lived experience of
*sad love* – love that defies the assumption that love stories
end in "happy ever after." Sad love in our songs and stories
tends to be a failure condition: a disaster and a tragedy. But
I think there is much more to it than that. The realities of
sad love are a clue that we're not seeing something properly.
Something is missed because we tell only certain kinds of
love stories. Sad love can't be happy ever after, of course.
But it can be something else: something that I'll call *eudaimonic* (more on this word a moment). Eudaimonic love has
deep connections with creativity and meaningfulness, of a
kind that the search for happy ever after doesn't and could
never have.

But who is this "us" I keep talking about? Words like "us"
can be sneaky. Unless we're paying attention, "us" tends
tacitly to exclude a "them." A simple word can mask swathes
of assumptions about who one is writing *for*, who's included
and who's excluded, who's normal and who's "other."

For the purposes of this book, "us" means me and the
people in the same boat as me, as far as romantic ideology goes. It means people who were fed the same cultural
soup that I was raised on, who imbibed the same "received
wisdom" about what (real) romantic love is. In the broad-
est terms, it's those of us who grew up with the dominant
(white, patriarchal, capitalistic and colonial) culture of
North America and the UK serving as our baseline world-
view. That's a vague and messy way to define an intended
audience, but the vagueness is intentional. It's the only way
to capture the group I have in mind, which is itself vague.
This book is about – and for – those of us who are still
swimming in that soup.

Much of the soup is made of stories. And our love stories are remarkably consistent, almost as if we are just telling one story over and over. Here's the short-form version of it:

> X and Y sitting in a tree,
> K-I-S-S-I-N-G.
> First comes love, then comes marriage,
> then comes baby in a baby carriage.

We teach this story to children. We teach them very early, before they are equipped with adult critical thinking, bullshit detectors, defensive armour of the mind. We feed kids this story, this bit of cultural soup, in simple rhyming packages, and that makes it easy for them to swallow and repeat to others. They receive it over and over again in fairy tales and stories and in snatches of adult culture – romcoms, romance novels, Valentine's Day greetings cards. And, of course, children watch grown-ups, and grown-ups model the story. We are supposed to start living out the story when we come of age, or at least do our darnedest to conform. For the children. If we cannot or will not conform, we *aren't supposed to let the children see that*.

It reminds me of something Wittgenstein said about rules: we just keep going. We call that "following" the rule. But, however it might feel from the inside, we're not really "following" anything. The way we go on is not determined by pre-existing constraints: it's up to us. We are creating the rule by going on the way we do.

I don't think all rules work this way, but a lot of them do.[1] In particular, most of our "rules" for romantic love are created by our own choices about how to go on, individually and in social groups. By practicing love in a particular way, by representing it as being that way, we are constructing the rules and norms and expectations for what a loving relationship should look like. We teach all of this to children. We keep going, and call that "on." It's not only about creating the rule, it's also about creating the "us."

It doesn't stop when we grow up, of course. The cultural messaging comes blaring at us all the time. It comes in at us from every direction and can occupy any and every available medium: magazines, news, music, friends, colleagues, family members. Anything can become an avatar, a conveyance of cultural soup. (Have you ever noticed how much text is on display in your bathroom while you are brushing your teeth?)

We cannot exactly tune all this out, but we can stop paying conscious attention. Indeed we *have* to stop paying conscious attention, because we have to use our attention – that limited and precious resource – for other things. So most of the time we just let the messaging wash over us, and it seeps into our subconscious unchecked. This makes it even more powerful: the less attention we pay to all these messages hiding in plain sight, the more easily they reach into the most intimate parts of our lives. (These days, I wear underpants only from the company that advertises on all my favourite podcasts.)

But let's tune in for a moment: let's pay some conscious attention. There's more than just stories in the soup. There's also received wisdom. For now, I'm not going to analyze or critique this. I just want to lay it out, as cleanly and simply as possible.

1 A good life is one full of love and happiness. A bad life is one with neither.
2 Love and happiness (the best things in life) are "free."
3 In order to live a good life, one should *pursue* love and happiness (as opposed to crass things such as wealth, power or fame).

These three messages may sound very familiar and homey. Perhaps they seem "obvious." But my hope, in writing them out so starkly here, is that I can begin to defamiliarize them a little bit. What might we think of these messages if they were entirely new to us? If we were strangers to the social world they define?

When you listen in to that third message, the one about what one should do in order to live a good life, you might hear some moralistic overtones. Something like: it is *unethical* to pursue money, power and fame. That's what *evil* people do. But in this context I am calling attention to message number three, not as an ethical proposition, but as a piece of strategic advice. A "good life" in this context is not necessarily an *ethical* life but the kind of life that is *good for the person living it*. The kind of life we would wish on our friends, or that a loving parent wants for their child. That's what I'm homing in on here. And, in the context of the first two messages, we can see how the third message makes sense as strategic advice. If you want a good life, you've got to pursue the things that *constitute* a good life, right?

The messages might strike us at first as simply discouraging avarice. We are advised to replace the pursuit of worldly goods with that of immaterial, abstract things. But it's not that simple. There may be ways to live a good life that do not involve the pursuit of any of these things. Indeed, that's where I think eudaimonia comes in. But, before we go there, let's take a look at where sad love fits into this cultural soup.

Sad love is all over the lyrics of popular music. Think of U2, for instance: "I can't live with or without you." Or Nine Inch Nails: "I hurt myself today, / To see if I still feel. / I focus on the pain, / The only thing that's real." Or Amy Winehouse: "We only said goodbye with words. / I died a hundred times. / You go back to her, / And I go back to / Black, black, black, black, black, black, black." Sociologist Thomas Scheff makes a case, in his 2011 book *What's Love Got to Do with It*, that pop music's image of love has been trending negative since at least the 1930s, with more and more songs depicting it as overwhelming and intensely painful (as well as self-centered and alienating). I largely agree with him that love as depicted in popular music is an extreme of feeling: either intense, ecstatic happiness or excruciating longing, loss and desperation. And that it's more usually the latter.

It's not just pop music that's obsessed with tragically sad love, though. The same thing occurs all over so-called high culture as well. Doomed, disastrous love drives the entire plot of classic novels such as *Anna Karenina* or *Wuthering Heights* and operas such as *La Bohème* and *La Traviata*. Juliet immediately wants to die when she finds out she can't be with Romeo, and vice versa.

This, then, is sad love as we collectively imagine it through our songs and stories: a failure condition. Never mediocre or boring, but spectacular and devastating and explosive. Not the daily grind of greyscale depression, but a melodramatic tragedy in gloriously (if horribly) intense technicolor, or . . ., well, black. We aren't presented with a subtle range of experiences. It's as if there are only two love stories: one a blissful fairy tale and the other a *total, utter tragedy*.

Notice, too, that these two stories have a lot in common: tragic love and happy ever after love are all about intense *feelings*, whether those feelings are positive or negative. Sadness and happiness are positioned at opposite ends of a scale for evaluating an individual's state of mind, from positive (happy) at one end to negative (sad) at the other.

Art and life are not so very separate from each other. Popular songs and classic novels wouldn't *be* popular and classic unless they resonated with millions of people. In fact, there is a tight circle of mutual influence between the two. The fact that life influences art is somewhat obvious: these songs are intentionally written to speak to as many people as possible and connect to their real (if extreme) emotional experiences.

The less obvious – but equally important – fact is that art influences life too. I argued in *What Love Is* that the socially constructed aspect of romantic love can be thought of as akin to a composite image. If you compile thousands of depictions of a face, the features they share in common emerge in the composite image as clearly defined contours. In just the same way, as we keep piling up our cultural representations of love, the features they share in common emerge from the composite image as clear features of love. These features can (and do) go on to shape a stereotype of what love looks like and a kind of script that we are expected to follow.

As a consequence, the ways we represent love as "happy" or "sad" can exert a powerful influence, not just on what we expect (from ourselves and others), in the sense of what we anticipate, but also on what we expect in a more normative sense: which kinds of love are socially acceptable and which are stigmatized or disfavoured. For instance, consider the power of representing queer love in movies or on TV. If we never see such love represented at all, we may have no conception of its being so much as possible. If we see queer love represented, but only between ridiculous or stereotyped characters, we are encouraged to distance ourselves from it and to laugh at it. What happens if we see queer love represented but only as *sad*?

Think of it this way: these composite images – stereotypes – generated by our cultural representations of love serve as a kind of roadmap for life. If the only road we can see that leads to "happy ever after" is the one labelled "Normal Relationship," we are discouraged from taking any other road. And not only that, but we are also subtly manipulated into dissuading our friends or family members from trying a different route. After all, we don't want the people we care about to be miserable.

While it makes for good art, tragic love is not supposed to be anybody's idea of a good *life*. When we say that "a good life is full of love," we don't mean a good life is full of Romeo and Juliet style suffering and suicidal despair. We mean that a good life is one full of *happy ever after* love.

It's OK for real-life love stories to be sad and dramatic for a little while, as the "protagonists" overcome some initial obstacles to their union, but, in a good life, that process should resolve before too long into a happy ever after relationship.

I'm not trying to suggest there is something intrinsically wrong with the fairy-tale romantic story (boy meets girl, etc., etc., and they lived happily ever after). That's a perfectly fine story, and a life that looks that way can be a perfectly good life. The problem is just that, if we tell the same story over and over, without telling any others, it becomes not just a story but a *script*, or a norm. And, once it's reached that status, it can be weaponized. It can be policed. Go off-script, and you are made to suffer. This is one reason why our stories matter so much. Being a social construct, our stereotype of romantic love is in a sense "made up": it's grounded in our fictions and fantasies, and these stories play a crucial part in maintaining its cultural dominance. But that doesn't mean there is nothing real going on here and nothing dangerous about it. The socially constructed norms of romantic love are "made up," but not in the same way that Sherlock Holmes is made up. It's more akin to how the *law* is made up. Sure, we made it up, but now it's real and you'd better treat it as such.

As I see it, however, romantic love is not simply a social construct. I think it has a dual nature: it's part social construct, part biology. Romantic love has a biological aspect in the sense that it does things to our brains and to our bodies. Love is in that respect quite a concrete, tangible thing, grounded in our evolutionary origins, susceptible to scientific study. It also has a socially constructed aspect, comprised of scripts and rules and traditions and expectations. These things are powerful[2] (just like biology is), but they shift as quickly as our values do, so love's socially constructed nature is best understood not by reaching back into our evolutionary past but by taking a well-informed look at our contextual present and our relatively recent history.

The relationship between love's biology and its socially constructed nature, or so I argued in *What Love Is*, is like that of an actor playing a role. It's as if we took certain ancient, evolved biological machinery and cast it to play the (heavily scripted) role of "romantic love" in a show called "Modern Society." We expect our brains and our bodies to *perform* in certain ways. We don't, as a rule, question the casting decision.

This book continues to focus attention on romantic love, so perhaps a word is in order about why. It's not because I think romantic love is the most important kind of love. Far from it. It's because romantic love is where I see all the most urgent philosophical problems boiling over. The romantic ideal and its accompanying romantic ideology are, in every sense of the word, *problematic*.

Many of the problems are in fact clustered around the idea that romantic love is the most important kind of love. The word "amatonormativity" was coined by philosopher Elizabeth Brake in 2011[3] to refer to the idea that it's normal and desirable for every adult to be in a romantic love relationship (of the "normal" – monogamous, permanent, marriage-like – kind), and that a normal person's life will be *centered* around that relationship, that it is the most important kind of relationship. Amatonormativity positions romantic love as special, as naturally taking precedence over all other connections to family, friends or community. The "plus one" you're expected to bring to an event is a romantic partner – or at least a prospective one, a "date" – not a sibling or a friend. The same goes for who you're expected to "settle down" and set up a home with. These assumptions are rarely spoken out loud, but they are everywhere, and they form the backdrop to all our decision-making. That's not to say we can't contravene them but that, if we do so, we'll be defying expectations.

Amatonormativity itself didn't pop into existence in 2011; the phenomenon is much older than its name. But a name is a powerful thing. Once we can name it, we have a handle on it. It's time we got a grip. Amatonormativity is not just old. It's a *tradition*, which is a far more serious matter. Traditions can run deep, to the core of our selves, informing our identities in complex ways.[4] The cultural practices with which we identify help to shape our sense of who we are, where we come from, which people are our people, and (of course) how our people do things. As a child, I learned how *my people* do love, and that, like it or not, became part of how I understood myself.

There is, then, a fourth piece of "received wisdom" that I want to add to the previous three. While amatonormativity is a complex and multifaceted phenomenon, the element of it that I want to focus attention on is simple:

4 Romantic love is the most important kind of love.

Again, for now I just want us to notice it and wonder about how it might strike us if it weren't already such a well-ensconced baseline expectation.

Let me round out this introduction with a summary guide to the rest of this book. To lay my cards on the table, the book's primary agenda is to urge that we replace the *romantic* conception of love with a *eudaimonic* conception. The romantic conception aims at an ideal (not realistic, but idealized) "happy ever after" – that is to say, a state that is pleasant for the individuals involved and is permanent. This ideal is what our current ideas about marriage are modelled on: monogamous and (mostly) heteronormative, and hence conducive to the creation of nuclear families which are culturally idealized as the locus of the happiest and most permanent kind of love. By contrast, the *eudaimonic* conception of love ditches the focus on pleasure (or "happiness") and orients instead towards meaningful, creative co-operation and collaboration.

This can occur in a wide range of forms and configurations, not all of which look like the nuclear family structure.

My understanding of what eudaimonic love is, and why it matters, came about through thinking about sad love. I called this book *Sad Love* for that reason. Sad love was my intellectual spark because it spoke back to romantic ideology so directly, demanding that I pay attention to the "happy" in the happy ever after and ask why it's there, what it's doing, and what is left of love when it goes away. But my goal isn't merely to talk about sad love or sadness *per se*. I am trying to frame a conception of love in which sadness has a role to play as something other than a failure condition. A eudaimonic conception of love has room for the full range of human experience, because it isn't oriented towards the "positive" emotions.

I will argue that the contemporary romantic ideal tends to make us miserable. But there are insights to be drawn from a close look at *why* that is the case and, indeed, why it's actually a predictable result given what we already know about how humans work. That's where I'll start in chapter 1. One thing philosophers have been trying to tell us for a long time is that, when we are deliberately trying to make ourselves happy – that is, when we are pursuing happiness for its own sake – it doesn't work. This is what's known as the Paradox of Happiness. This first chapter also surveys the contemporary context, against which this old philosophical idea sits somewhat awkwardly: North American positivity culture positions individualistic happiness as a core ideal, and the "pursuit of happiness" is baked right into the dominant ideology of my time and place. Against this, the Paradox of Happiness emerges as an important clue about who and what we are. It suggests important failings in a positivity-oriented culture, which will turn out to have analogues in the context of romance.

Chapter 2 begins by tracing out those analogies. I argue that, just as pursuing happiness doesn't work, pursuing the romantic *happy ever after* doesn't work either. In fact this, too, tends to make us miserable. I call this the Romantic Paradox.

In chapter 3, I discuss a well-known response to the Paradox of Happiness, which I think will also help us with the Romantic Paradox. This response requires us to distinguish happiness from something else. The "something else" is often called *eudaimonia*, which tends to be translated as "flourishing" or "well-being." And so the classic resolution to the Paradox of Happiness, then, is to recognize that eudaimonia is more important than happiness and to engage in activities that promote eudaimonia (which may, as a side benefit, bring happiness in its wake).

It's one thing, however, to appreciate that eudaimonia is different from happiness. It's another – much tougher – thing to say what eudaimonia *is*. The concept of eudaimonia is ancient and is generally associated with the philosophy of Aristotle. But he didn't invent it.[5] In any case, we have all kinds of tools at our disposal now for sharpening the concept that Aristotle didn't have, such as twentieth-century literature and contemporary empirical research. Conceptions of eudaimonia inspired by Aristotle do not appeal to me, and some of his ideas about "human flourishing" all too easily spill over into ableism, or even eugenics. So in the remainder of chapter 3 I take up some of the tools available to me and try to fashion a very different conception of eudaimonia.

I take my cue from the etymology of the word *eudaimonia*, calling attention to the *daimons* – literally, "spirits" – that shape our loves, and indeed our lives. Daimons don't have to be understood as literally supernatural, but the daimon metaphor can be extremely useful for thinking about everything from an individual's "vibe" to the environment of a workplace, the spirit of a nation state, or the intangible presence of capitalism in our lives.

Chapter 4 brings further ingredients into the mix that I will use to expand upon what eudaimonic love is. It begins by surveying some of the (serious) methodological challenges that face anyone trying to understand love and happiness, which I try to locate in the context of general difficulties with "knowing ourselves." This leads into a conception of who and what we are that draws from existentialist philosophical traditions, emphasizing our agency in the process of creating ourselves.

This in turn can be applied to help me explain how eudaimonic love differs from romantic love, to which I turn in chapter 5. One of the most important differences is that eudaimonic love is active and dynamic, while romantic conceptions are typically passive and static. In the romantic framework we talk about "falling" in love, as if it were something that simply happened to us, like falling into a pit. Or being struck by a bolt of lightning (another common romantic metaphor). In eudaimonic love we choose our own way, guided by what makes our lives and our projects meaningful. Such choices are constrained by circumstances and the choices of others, but I understand these constraints by analogy with the role of constraints in artistic creativity. I also draw on research concerning "job-crafting" (a process by which employees craft their roles, adding to or even going against their job descriptions) to develop an analogous notion of "love-crafting," which is the creative practice of tailoring loving relationships to the skills, needs and values of the people in them.

Ultimately, I argue, we need to stop hearing "romantic" as a positive description. It's actually something that should raise a sceptical eyebrow. I urge that we move towards understanding *ideal* love as eudaimonic, not romantic. I also think we would do well to stop thinking so much about whether our partners "make us happy" and focus instead on whether they lovingly collaborate with us in the co-creation of meaningful work, and of our selves.

That, then, is this book's destination. Its starting point is a conversation I had a few years ago, with my American husband, about "the pursuit of happiness" . . .

# 1

# The Paradox of Happiness

## As dreamers do

Like me, my husband Jonathan is a philosophy professor. We sometimes talk shop together. When I was working on this book, I talked with Jonathan about love, and sadness, and the idea of being "happy ever after."

One day, I mentioned to him in passing that "the pursuit of happiness" struck me as a very American thing. He was surprised to hear that I thought so.

"Isn't that basically the same everywhere?" he asked.

I was surprised by his surprise. Jonathan is an American citizen, but he isn't the kind of stereotypical American who imagines the world beyond the contiguous United States to be a vague blur of terrorists and starving children. He reads, he travels, he's lived in Scotland, and now he lives with me in Canada. He's a pretty worldly-wise, generally cool human. Why would he assume everywhere is like America?

I had to stop and think about his question. In fact, I haven't really stopped thinking about it ever since. Gradually, I came to the conclusion that Jonathan was right. The pursuit of happiness *is* everywhere. But I was right too. I'm going to try and untangle some different strands in this question, and then I think that will make sense.

The phrasing "the pursuit of happiness" has specifically American roots. It appears most famously in the 1776 US Declaration of Independence: "We hold these truths to be self-evident, that all men are created equal, that they are endowed by their Creator with certain unalienable Rights, that among these are Life, Liberty and the pursuit of

Happiness."[1] These ideals and this specific way of expressing them are built into the USA's origin story – or, more accurately, the story it tells about its origins. They lie at the core of the nation's identity – or, more accurately, its self-image. The USA counts its very existence as beginning in 1776 with this declaration, rather than in 1781 with the ratification of Articles of Confederation. There is something *about* the Declaration of Independence. Somehow it is more existential, more constitutive of the nation's sense of itself, than even the document that literally constituted the uniting of the United States.

When I see all those tee-shirts insisting on "Good Vibes Only" or carefully curated Instagram feeds telling me to "Find Joy in Every Moment," it's interesting to contextualize these things by remembering that American happiness culture got started as soon as America did.

Still, Jonathan was not wrong about its universality. One might encounter ideas like these more or less anywhere nowadays. But I think that to a large extent that is true because American ideas and ideals have been exported to the rest of the world. The increasing homogeneity of global culture is linked to America's geopolitical dominance.

It certainly feels to me as if happiness ideology has been on the rise over the course of my lifetime. I don't remember happiness being nearly so prominent when I was growing up in a lower-middle-class British household in the 1980s and 1990s. I recall a cultural focus on underdogs, pessimism, left-wing political satire, and toilet humour.

And I'm not alone in thinking things used to be different. Happiness culture *used* to be specifically American. In *Man's Search for Meaning*,[2] Austrian psychiatrist and Holocaust survivor Viktor Frankl wrote: "To the European, it is a characteristic of the American culture that, again and again, one is commanded and ordered to 'be happy'."

There have been some significant developments in American happiness culture since 1776. Ideas about happiness being *healthy* – or perhaps even *the same thing* as health – arrive on the scene by 1902, when American philosopher William James declares that a "healthy-minded" individual is one who has that "tendency which looks on all things and sees that they are good." (Those for whom "the world . . . looks remote, strange, sinister and uncanny," for whom "its colour is gone and its breath is cold," are labelled by James as "sick souls.")[3]

Even more significantly – for my purposes in this book – there is a strand in this culture that says all you need to do to achieve your goals in life is to think happy thoughts. That everything you most desire will come to you through the power of *positive thinking*.

Perhaps you've heard of a book called *The Secret* (based on a film of the same name). Oprah Winfrey is a big fan. First published in 2006, it's sold over 30 million copies worldwide. Even if you haven't heard of *The Secret* by name, you might have heard of the "law of attraction" that it popularized.[4] This "law" says that you can "manifest" things in your life just by having corresponding thoughts.

Proponents of the law of attraction compare people to magnets. You can become a money magnet – manifest money just by thinking about having lots of money. Or you can become a love magnet, or a Rolex magnet, or a CEO job magnet, or whatever. You just need to *feel yourself already having* the thing you want, and it will come to you. If you feel rich, you'll be rich. If you feel lucky in love, you'll be lucky in love. On the other hand, feeling like a loser is a self-fulfilling prophecy. Just as positive thoughts manifest positive results, negative thoughts manifest negative results because "like attracts like." (This is literally the opposite of how magnets work, but let's not quibble over details.) The basic metaphysical claim of *The Secret* is that reality will conform itself to the way you think of it, as opposed to what is commonly assumed: that we should try to conform our beliefs to reality.

The idea that convincing yourself you're rich and beloved is all it takes for money and love to "manifest" in your life might sound delusional to some. But we should tread carefully here. This seems, for many people, to be a genuinely held belief. And millions are at least sufficiently interested in the idea to shell out the price of a book.

Moreover, it's not as if the law of attraction just arrived out of the blue in 2006. The American Dream has long sold what is, in many ways, a watered-down version of the same story: that anyone can make it in America. Anyone can be "self-made," pull themselves up by their bootstraps, start out with nothing and become a millionaire or a president or an astronaut.

A crucial part of both the American Dream and the law of attraction is that it doesn't matter if you start out with nothing. It doesn't matter who you are or what you have, and you don't need to rely on anyone else's help. You individually can get where you want to be, *provided you make the effort.* The only difference is that, where the American Dream says you get what you want through certain kinds of hard work, the law of attraction says you get it through certain kinds of positive thinking.

As you might suspect by now, I am not even a little bit sympathetic to either of these claims. Nobody accomplishes anything without support and co-operation. Wealth is dramatically correlated with markers of privilege, especially race,[5] and so are dating preferences.[6] Those who start with nothing have little chance of "succeeding" materially in America, while, by the same measure, those who start life as billionaires are hard pressed to do anything that wouldn't count as "success."

The way I see it, the American Dream was already so thoroughly disconnected from the realities of how power works and how a society functions that, for people who'd already bought into *that* mythology, the law of attraction was an easy sell. It might be delusional, but it's the kind of delusion that's a natural and continuous next step from where America already was.

Do you remember Jiminy Cricket's song from the 1940 Disney classic, *Pinocchio*? It begins "When you wish upon a star . . ." and promises that absolutely anything can be attained through this method. Sounds a bit like *The Secret*, don't you think? When I say there were forerunners to the law of attraction, helping to pry open the chasm between American Dreams and reality, this is the kind of thing I mean.

In "When you wish upon a star," there are literally no limits to what you can acquire: "anything your heart desires," it promises, "will come to you." And perhaps even more importantly, anybody can acquire these things: it "makes no difference who you are," provided only that "your heart is in your dreams." As in all versions of the American Dream, it doesn't matter if you start out with nothing. We don't have to worry about correcting for any inequalities in people's starting positions, or redistributing, or levelling the playing field. (To the stereotypical American, all that sort of talk sounds like communism, which is to say it sounds heinous.)

But you might be tempted to think: *So what? It's just a kids' song performed by a cartoon insect.* But it really isn't just that. It has become an icon. It is now symbolic of the entire Disney brand (a snippet from this song is played when the logo appears at the start of any Disney movie), and Disney, in turn, has become a kind of avatar for American culture writ large. This is a song that matters. It *means* something.

I'm not the only one who thinks so: in 2009 (right around the time *The Secret* came out, as it happens), "When you wish upon a star" was inducted into the National Recording Registry. That's a Library of Congress collection of recordings that "are culturally, historically, or aesthetically important, and/or inform or reflect life in the United States." The question is not whether this song is a big deal but, rather, what becomes of a culture when fully grown adults are buying into this kind of thing to the extreme degree evinced by the runaway success of *The Secret*.

Eventually, the idea that you can make something true just by treating it as if it's already true really does become delusional. You'll start thinking you're at liberty, at any time, to choose your own preferred set of "alternative facts"[7] and treat them as the truth. And that doing so will ensure that they *become* the truth. Is it surprising, then, that eventually an American president feels as if he need only keep *saying* and *acting as if* he has won the presidential election in order to "manifest" the desired victory? Donald Trump, like Disney, has only been another avatar of the American Dream culture. Losing touch with reality is on brand.

One of the most important ways in which the Dream encourages us to lose touch with reality is by focusing all our attention on individuals and what they can do on their own. Wishing on stars and attempting to manifest one's desires through positive thinking are individualistic acts, and looking to them distracts us from co-operative or co-ordinated actions we might undertake with others. I'll have much more to say about this as we go along.

## Happiness cannot be pursued

Remember Viktor Frankl, who said in 1946: "it is a characteristic of the American culture that, again and again, one is commanded and ordered to 'be happy'"? Well, he went on to add: "But happiness cannot be pursued; it must ensue." That is a snappy summary of an old problem known as the *Paradox of Happiness*.

Another statement of the same paradox can be found in the writings of English philosopher John Stuart Mill. Mill was an ethicist and political philosopher, and these days he is most famous for his defense of utilitarianism (the view that the best thing to do in any given scenario is whatever will produce the greatest happiness for the greatest number).[8] But, in 1873, he also wrote this:

> Those only are happy ... who have their minds fixed on some object other than their own happiness; on the happiness of others, on the improvement of mankind, even on some art or pursuit, followed not as a means, but as itself an ideal end. Aiming thus at something else, they find happiness by the way.[9]

This is really quite similar to the conclusion that Frankl would come to, some seventy years later, after World War II. Mill is saying that, if you *try* to be happy, you won't be happy. You have to aim at something else. Happiness "cannot be pursued." That, in a nutshell, is the Paradox of Happiness.

The word *paradox* derives from ancient Greek words for beyond (*para*) and belief (*doxa*). A paradox is something that is beyond belief, or very surprising, and usually not in a good way. The word is generally used to refer to problems that don't have any obvious solution. I tend to think of paradoxes as intellectual problems that can't be solved without letting go of something we were clinging to, something big. Something that perhaps strikes us as *too big to fail*. In that sense, paradoxes can often reveal to us where our intellectual foundations are wrong.

The Paradox of Happiness is like that, I think. Its lesson is that we need to change something about our ways of thinking, but the changes required run so deep that they are almost unimaginable. Resolutions have been proposed, but for one reason or another they have had a hard time getting the majority of us to buy into them.

Mill himself offered some guidance on what to do in light of the Paradox of Happiness. In the passage above, he suggests that, since trying to be happy doesn't work, you should stop trying. Aim at some *other* goal in life, then happiness will emerge as a by-product. It's almost as if we have to imagine happiness as one of those dim, twinkling stars that you can only see out of the corner of your eye: if you set your sights right at it, it immediately disappears. But, as long as you're resolutely looking somewhere else, you can be vaguely aware of it.

But let's be real: that's weird, confusing, *frustrating* advice. Taken in combination with the culturally dominant idea that happiness and the romantic "happy ever after" are definitive of a good life, it seems practically useless. How are we supposed to believe that some X is the best thing in life and *also not try to achieve X*?

I think the problem presented by the Paradox of Happiness is actually getting worse over time. Given that the *pursuit* of happiness – once a distinctively American value – has gone global, the *Paradox* of Happiness is now more or less everyone's problem. (Intriguingly, though, there are still some observable differences between the USA and other parts of the world. For example, recent research[10] found that Russian parents are more likely to read their children stories involving "negative" emotions, and more likely to value those emotions, than American parents.) J. S. Mill made one suggestion about how to deal with the Paradox, but he was a nineteenth-century private gentleman scholar offering us an unsubstantiated solution with no clinical or empirical backing. Don't we have anything better yet?

Not really. We do have several versions of the *same* suggestion, give or take a few bells and whistles. The Paradox of Happiness will pop its head over the parapet every so often in philosophical conversations, with a number of different variations emerging over the years.[11] But the resolutions are mostly quite similar to Mill's.

Part of the response has to be a nuanced critique of the idea that life is (or should be) all about the pursuit of happiness. The associated "positivity culture" that has come to be dominant in North American society also needs to be tackled if any resolution is to gain serious traction. In some circles, "toxic positivity" is starting to catch on as a handy phrase to refer to a misguided focus on the positive to the exclusion of all else. But the phrase is not exactly on the tip of everyone's tongue just yet. As of the end of December 2020, Googling "toxic positivity" turned up about 528,000 results. (For comparison, "toxic masculinity" yielded about 2,490,000.)

Still, this critical project has a long history, with some rich slices that we can dig into for inspiration. In the satirical novella *Candide, ou L'Optimisme*, published in 1759, the French philosopher Voltaire ridicules the idea that we live in "the best of all possible worlds." In *Candide*, a fictional philosopher called Pangloss persistently tries to argue that "all is for the best": that our world is the best world God could possibly have created. This is a response to the problem of evil (a philosophical problem which challenges Christian theologists to account for suffering in a world created by a loving omnipotent God). The simplistic defense offered by Pangloss is made to look silly and naïve, and the absurdity of it becomes more and more apparent over the course of the novella as he argues that murder, war, disease, earthquakes, and even syphilis are desirable features of our world.

Interestingly, *Candide* was written even before the American Declaration of Independence. However, it is generally thought to be a critical response to the earlier German philosopher Leibniz, and Leibniz – writing back in the early 1700s – is plausibly the source inspiration for the idea that the pursuit of happiness is among the natural rights of "all men" found in the declaration. In many ways, Voltaire was already critiquing positivity culture even before it was cool. If you wince at bumper stickers telling you to "See the best in everything," you're not alone. Voltaire is on your side.

*Candide* is good satire, but it's not much more than that. It's not by itself a compelling resolution to the Paradox of Happiness.

Viktor Frankl gives us a bit more to go on. Frankl published *Man's Search for Meaning* in 1946, after the end of World War II. As well as saying that "happiness cannot be pursued," he recommends that we focus, not on happiness, but on whatever makes life *meaningful* for us. Frankl is basing his conclusions on his direct observations of life in a Nazi concentration camp, and specifically who survived and who did not. In circumstances where happiness was no longer possible, some prisoners were able to orient their lives towards something else – something meaningful, such as a beloved person or a creative goal. The people who did this, Frankl argues, had a much better chance of survival than those who didn't. That convinced him that it was meaning, not happiness, that really mattered. I'll have more to say about this idea throughout the rest of this book.

Coming closer to the present, we start to get some empirical data from psychologists investigating the Paradox of Happiness. In 2011, results were published from a series of experiments in which researchers looked for associations between how much their subjects said they *valued* happiness and how happy those same subjects actually *were*. They found that "[v]aluing happiness was associated with lower hedonic balance, lower psychological well-being, less satisfaction with life, and higher levels of depression symptoms."[12] As they summarize things: "valuing happiness could be self-defeating." Set your sights on happiness and you end up with just the opposite. This sounds just like what Mill or Frankl would have predicted.

There's another point about this experimental work that's worth pausing over here, too. In their paper the study authors use the phrase "hedonic balance" as a kind of proxy for happiness. But what precisely is "hedonic balance"? They explain: "Because our scale needed to correspond to the present, western cultural context, we equated happiness to a prominent definition in this context: an individual's positive hedonic state." "Hedonic" is derived from an ancient Greek word, *hedone*, meaning pleasure or nice feelings. "Hedonic" (as in "hedonism") refers to something which feels good. Something pleasant and positive. To me, this is an important reflection of the social context in which the research takes place. In a nutshell, what the researchers are saying is that they are equating happiness with pleasurable feelings. And they're doing so in order to keep their research in line with how happiness is defined in "the present, western cultural context."

In other words, they'll define happiness as pleasure because *that's what people around here think happiness is.*

And, of course, this doesn't come out of nowhere. In 1874, another English philosopher called Henry Sidgwick described a problem that is, in essence, another version of the Paradox of Happiness. Sidgwick writes: "Here comes into view what we might call the fundamental paradox of Hedonism, that the impulse towards pleasure, if too predominant, defeats its own aim."[13] The "impulse towards pleasure" is much the same thing as the "pursuit of happiness," once happiness and pleasure are equated (as they eventually will be by our "western cultural context"). And, in saying that chasing after pleasure is a self-defeating exercise, Sidgwick is making just the same point as Mill, Frankl and the psychologists.

What could it mean for the impulse towards pleasure to be "too predominant"? Is it pleasure itself that's causing the problem, or is it specifically the focus on *one's own* pleasure? Can we solve the paradox by focusing on someone else's pleasure? If so, this might suggest a way out of the paradox that is different from Frankl's. Frankl says we must do the (harder and more confusing) work of orienting ourselves towards something meaningful. Someone else's pleasure is, by contrast, a relatively concrete, obvious goal to adopt.

As I think about that option, it calls to my mind the way in which *women* in particular are expected to put the pleasure of others first, especially in heterosexual contexts.[14] Jess

Phillips, writing about this issue for *The Guardian*, captures my memories of teenage sexuality in the UK perfectly:

> When they were touching us and we were gloating about it, we garnered zero pleasure from such interactions – beyond getting to tell your mates that the fittest one had stuck his hand in your knickers. . . . No one ever told us that it would be great if you liked each other, better if you did it because you actually got off from it. Bless the boys, I think they thought we enjoyed it. No one told them, either. . . . We were vessels for the boys' exploration. No one ever said that sex was for us, too.[15]

In a twisted alternative to the rampant slut-shaming that (as I came to understand only much later) coloured North American contexts during the same time period, what I experienced was something like a constant pressure to provide pleasure without ever expecting to get any.

What does this have to do with the Paradox of Happiness? Well, one thing it suggests is that the solution can't be quite as simple as needing to stop focusing on our own pleasures and start focusing on someone else's, or else sexually exploratory teenage British girls in the 1990s should have been the epitome of human happiness. (Spoiler: we were not.)

### I give myself very good advice (but I very seldom follow it)

There's one last Paradox of Happiness I want to talk about to round off this chapter, both because it helps us complete our map of the problem and because it gives us more pointers as to where the (genuine) routes out of the quagmire lie. This is not the same paradox we've been talking about up until now, but it's connected, as a many-headed hydra is connected at the torso.

The snappy summary of this paradox is that, even if people *know* what to do in order to be happy, they still don't do it. There is quite a lot of information out there these days on how to be happy: empirical research, time-tested advice, and a steady stream of best-selling self-help books on the subject.[16] And a lot of this advice points the same way: it tells us that happiness comes with engaging actively in projects that point beyond ourselves – helping other people, developing deep skills, or engaging in creative projects. Long-term, robust happiness is particularly associated with what are now known as "flow" activities – activities that typically require (physical and/or mental) effort to get started but once underway capture our attention and imaginations completely and generate experiences of well-being that cannot be replicated by passive or acquisitive experiences (aka binge-watching Netflix and purchasing items on Amazon).

Have you ever been completely "in the zone," working on something you are really into, something that absorbs all your attention, until you lose track of time? You snap out of it and realize that hours have passed in what felt like minutes, and you've achieved way more than you ever thought you would. This is often called the "flow" state. It can feel like magic or a kind of creative trance. A pioneering researcher of the flow state, positive psychologist Mihaly Csikszentmihalyi, gave an influential TED talk about it called "Flow, the secret to happiness."[17] Currently, it has over 6.7 million views.

In the talk, Csikszentmihalyi argues that it is *flow*, not fame or fortune, that makes us happy. He cites data indicating that the percentage of people in the United States who say they are "very happy" didn't change much from 1956 to 1998, even though income nearly tripled (after adjusting for inflation) in that time, and he summarizes a wealth of other research that seems to suggest that "increases in material well-being don't seem to affect how happy people are," provided people are decently over the poverty line.

This looks to be bringing us back to one of those pieces of received wisdom:

2 Love and happiness (the best things in life) are "free."

But we can push back against this interpretation with some more data. In a 2015 publication, the Office for National Statistics in the UK reported that "[a]n individual's level of personal well-being is strongly related to the level of wealth of the household in which they live. Life satisfaction, sense of worth and happiness are higher, and anxiety less, as the level of household wealth increases."[18]

A tempting knee-jerk response is to say that this kind of correlation must be about meeting basic needs for shelter and food. Naturally, it's hard to be happy if you lack those bare necessities. But, once those are provided for, surely getting more money beyond that point doesn't make us happier? As Csikszentmihalyi put it in his TED talk, "the lack of basic . . . material resources contributes to *un*happiness, but the increase in material resources [does] not increase happiness."

But no, as it turns out, it's not so simple. The claim that wealth level affects happiness only when it interferes with meeting our basic needs has been explicitly and deliberately tested in the US context. Correlations between wealth happiness were found across the entire range of income levels.[19]

OK – you might be thinking – maybe wealth and happiness are correlated. But that doesn't necessarily mean happiness costs money. It could be the other way around. Maybe it's not that money buys happiness, but that happiness attracts money! Indeed, Shawn Achor argues exactly this in *The Happiness Advantage*, published in 2010. For those who find the thesis of *The Secret* (that positive thinking alone can "manifest" money in your life) a bit "woo," *The Happiness Advantage* offers a more mundane explanation of a similar result: being happier means you will be more productive, hence more successful, hence richer.

But there are more spanners in the works, alas. Awkward data points that do not fit. One is that some studies suggest that in certain contexts *negative* attitudes predict success, while optimism leads to risky behaviour and failure. (A 2002 study reports that "there are times when pessimism and negative thinking . . . lead to better performance and personal growth.")[20] But even worse news is to be found in a 2017 paper called "Buying time promotes happiness." This paper investigates the effects of paying someone else to do one's unwanted tasks – such as cleaning or shopping – thus "buying back" the time these tasks would have taken up. The findings suggested that spending money this way was *not only* correlated with greater life satisfaction but actually caused it.[21]

But how can that be, if entering the flow state is what makes us happy, and that doesn't cost any money? There's the rub: it does! In fact, many flow-inducing activities *obviously* cost money: art supplies and pianos and hiking gear aren't free. But, even if we assume an activity itself is "free" to participate in, there is always going to be a cost in terms of lost time. If you have to work long hours and care for a family, you can't necessarily set aside an hour each day for yoga or martial arts. You aren't necessarily able to spend your evenings pursuing the artistic endeavours that set your imagination on fire. Under capitalism, time is money, and being able to spend one's time on flow activities is a marker of economic privilege.

Author Ruth Whippman, writing in *The Guardian* in 2016, calls the claim that money can't buy happiness a "fridge-magnet mantra" and "a cosy boast of our lack of materialism." Marshalling various studies and surveys, she sums matters up this way: "Money makes us happy! Suggesting otherwise doesn't make us spiritually enlightened or morally superior. It makes us clueless."[22] But even Whippman admits that "there are anomalies in the data." Money doesn't *automatically* make us happy. Whether money can buy happiness depends on how you spend it, and purchasing more and more expensive toys for yourself does not generally work. The truth is that, although money and happiness are related, this relationship can't be reduced to a catchphrase, whether it's *Money can't buy happiness!* or *Money makes us happy!*

When we get beyond the catchphrases, what seems to be a recurring factor is the role of *time*. To see why and how engaging in "flow" activities is a privilege, we have to appreciate that there is a "cost" to these activities in terms of time *not* spent on other things (such as working a second or third minimum-wage job). And, in thinking about how money can buy happiness, the most promising suggestion I know of is to spend it on buying time *back*.

Be all this as it may, we aren't exactly lacking in *information* on how to be happy. We may be denied the *opportunity* to follow the strategies best backed by research, of course. But there may be more to it than just that.

There was a paper published in 2017 called: "The paradox of happiness: why are we not doing what we know makes us happy?" In this paper, the researchers report finding that

> People know that flow activities facilitate happiness better than more passive leisure and yet they are not doing these activities because it seems they do not know how to overcome the activation energy or transition costs required to pursue true enjoyment. This disjunction perhaps leads us to assume that happiness is going to happen to us as an outcome of our pursuit of hedonism. Thus, we develop a more passive approach to happiness, opting for the easier pleasurable activities that require less energy and are less daunting than high-investment flow activities.[23]

As I see it, they're essentially arguing that seeking pleasure is never going to get us to step away from Netflix and stop ordering stuff from Amazon. Those activities *do* give us pleasure, and that pleasure comes easily, so why would we bother doing something hard?

The empirical support adduced by psychologists is new, but the basic idea here is not. Henry Sidgwick, back in the 1800s, was onto the very same thing. After introducing his "paradox of hedonism," he adds that

> [its] effect is not visible, or at any rate is scarcely visible, in the case of passive sensual pleasures. But of our active enjoyments generally, whether the activities on which they attend are classed as "bodily" or as "intellectual" (as well as of many emotional pleasures), it may certainly be said that we cannot attain them, at least in their highest degree, so long as we keep our main conscious aim concentrated upon them. It is not only that the exercise of our faculties is insufficiently stimulated by the mere desire of the pleasure attending it, and requires the presence of other more objective, "extra-regarding," impulses, in order to be fully developed: we may go further and say that these other impulses must be temporarily predominant and absorbing, if the exercise and its attendant gratification are to attain their full scope.

Although this idea has been around for a long time, in our culture at large it has lost out to the *pursuit of happiness* (understood in the contemporary way as pleasure and nice feelings). That's why recent research (and – let's be honest – daily experience) still finds us bingeing shows and shopping online.

If we want the kind of "true enjoyment" that comes from those "predominant and absorbing" or "high-investment" flow activities, we need to figure out how to deprogram ourselves: to *disengage* from the pursuit of happiness and all the baggage it brings with it.

Then, maybe, we'll have a better shot at understanding – *really* understanding – how to find happiness. And, more importantly, whether happiness was what we were looking for in the first place, in love or in any other aspect of life.

## The taming of happiness

"Happy" didn't always mean what it does now. We have to be careful using word meanings in philosophical enquiries. As every teacher knows, starting your essay with a dictionary definition rarely leads to a deep philosophical insight. In fact, with "happy," the dictionary might serve only to muddy the waters even further. Look up "happy" in the Oxford English Dictionary and, even ignoring the noun uses, you get different definitions for senses 1a, 1b, 2, 3, 4a, 4b, 5a, 5b, 5c, 5d, 5e, 6 and 7.[24] That said, the *history* of a word's meaning – the trunk that gave rise to all those current branches – can sometimes help us see a bigger picture, or take the long view, of what a word is up to.

I love etymology. I find it completely fascinating in its own right – it feels like reading a word's life story, and some words have lived incredible lives. But there's something else that draws me to the deep history of words, too. The echoes of a word's original meanings, even if we've now abandoned those meanings entirely, can give us clues about the evolution of the concepts behind the words: how we've been thinking of the things the words stand for. They can be especially useful as clues about where those concepts come from: the foundations on which they stand.

Could it be useful, then, to dig down into what our English word "happy" originally meant? Maybe. But, while I love etymology, we still have to be careful. It isn't going to provide a knock-down argument for any specific conclusion. Sometimes the clues etymology provides can be misleading. Often they are somewhat parochial, as languages themselves are. And sometimes etymology just doesn't deliver much of interest. So we'll proceed with caution. But let's see what's down there.

In the deep history of the word "happy" we turn up connections with luck, fate, chance, and the course of events. These things all used to be called "hap." To be called "happy" was, once upon a time, to be regarded as lucky or fortunate in terms of how things turned out for you. To "have good hap" meant to have good things happen to you: the word "happen" actually comes from the same root. Although the root word "hap" no longer survives, it is a prolific ancestor with a fascinating family tree, whose tendrils are spread out all our conversations about the mis*hap*s of the *hap*less and the *hap*hazard condition of life. The per*hap*s of it all.[25]

These days, we have sidelined the role of luck and circumstances in happiness. In fact, it's more common to hear the opposite kind of message: that happiness comes from within, that you are responsible for your own happiness.

"Happiness" is now more readily associated with being in a good mood, or with feeling positive, than with things such as chance or good luck. I think that there is a real clue that we've lost in forgetting about the role of luck – a clue about the deep problem giving rise to the Paradox of Happiness. To test that hunch, I'll need to try and pull that clue into the light. And, to do *that*, I need to talk for a while about how we understand happiness these days and draw out some points of comparison.

Nowadays, the study of happiness falls into the domain of "positive psychology": the study of "positive" ("good") states of mind. Happiness is often counted as one such state, and so is love – in fact, this is a very important point of connection between the two that I will have more to say about later.

For now, what matters is that, as a subdiscipline of psychology, positive psychology defines itself in opposition to the field's earlier focus on the *negative* – that is to say, on mental illnesses, problems and pathologies. All the ways our minds can go "wrong," in other words. Positive psychology isn't about curing psychological disease. Rather, it aims to understand the bright side of our mental lives. Our good feelings and positive experiences. Our mental wellness.

Positive psychology has been acknowledged as a subdiscipline for about twenty years, but it remains controversial in certain circles and has been accused of peddling toxic positivity. Some sceptics, such as Barbara Ehrenreich,[26] go so far as to argue that positive psychology is more of an ideological movement than an academic discipline, that it is supported by right-wing political powerhouses because it advances their conservative ends, and that it operates more on the model of the self-help market, or even a cult, than on that of a science.

Another critic, Ruth Whippman, titled a chapter of one of her books[27] "Positive psychology (or, if you're not happy, it's your own fault, you lazy schmuck)." In that chapter she interviews another author, Linda Tirado, who says: "positive thinking isn't just useless, it's counterproductive to my self-esteem . . . You cannot kick me and expect me to say thank you for kicking me with a smile on my face."

Many of these criticisms revolve around the worry that positive psychology has an ideological agenda: to convince us that positivity and negativity are under our control, that it's our *choice* whether or not to be happy.

I have some sympathy with this worry. The list of things I'm told I'm supposed to be doing in order to be happy – and to improve my "wellness" – seems to be endless. And focusing too much attention on that list certainly can have a dark side. It means we can always explain any suffering that we encounter by looking at what the suffering *individual* is or is not doing, without ever broaching structural questions about (say) systemic racism, colonialism, misogyny and poverty. Instead, the suffering individual can be held responsible for her own suffering. Perhaps she is not sufficiently grateful. She is not meditating enough. She is not eating well enough or exercising enough or building good enough friendships or reading the right books or following the right gurus or developing a growth mindset or acquiring enough resilience or cultivating "grit" … We can derail and distract from those awkward structural issues for ever if we go on like this.

And this all locks very neatly into place within the American Dream ideology. The original Dream promised each man (*sic*) that he could "make something of himself" in America, provided he was willing to work hard. That he was *entitled* to certain things – a middle-class home, wife and kids, various comforts and status markers – as long as he put the effort in. It's an ideology of optimistic economic individualism. Under positivity culture, this sense of what the deserving individual is entitled to plays out just the same way in the emotional realm. One is promised that the pursuit, not of wealth, but of *happiness* will deliver results. If you do your yoga class, eat healthy food, use your meditation app for ten minutes a day, and all the rest, you too can be happy. It's as if the pursuit of happiness has subtly shifted from being our inalienable *right* to being our *duty*.

Again, the assumption that everyone is in a position to achieve said results is absolutely crucial to the Dream ideology. This is where one of those three messages we looked at in the introduction comes into play. Happiness doesn't cost anything, and indeed cannot be bought, or so the message tells us. Thus there is no need to worry about wealth inequality, since it presents no barrier to universal happiness. (Don't worry, we'll be coming back to address *this* zinger of a claim in chapter 2.) Anyone who does the right things is *entitled* to be happy. Here is psychologist Paul Hewitt on this point: "There's a notion that you can expect to be happy. There's a sense of entitlement that goes along with that, too: *I'm supposed to be happy. If the world were fair, I would be happy. I should be happy.*" This version of the American Dream is not about economic status, at least not directly; it is about *emotional* status. I call it the Emotional Dream.

I deploy that concept of *status* here intentionally, with all its connotations of status anxiety, comparisons, and aspirations of "keeping up with the Joneses." Instead of just parking the right car in the driveway to prove to our nosey neighbours that we are *economically* successful, we also have to post enough smiley pictures on social media (hashtag-blessed, hashtag-gratitude) to prove to an entire online world of nosey neighbours that we are *emotionally* successful – that is to say, happy.

The moralistic tone of "the best things in life are free" pushes our attention away from the awkward, uncomfortable fact that, under capitalism, money is absolutely necessary for living a good, or even decent, life. The received wisdom creates an ideological smokescreen: *only love and happiness are really worth having*, we're told. *And therefore* (we are supposed to conclude) *nothing of real value is being denied to even the poorest people. As long as you are good, you will be loved and you will be happy.* And that, in turn, means there's nothing going wrong here: nothing needs to change. The Emotional Dream is – like all other versions of the American Dream, and for similar reasons – inherently small "c" conservative.

With all that said, it's not exactly easy to *object* to happiness *per se*, or to the scientific project of studying human minds in order to figure out how we can increase the amount of happiness in the world. And I'm not objecting to these things. While I feel the force of the objections to positivity culture, I do not propose that we *stop doing the science of happiness*. There is certainly some empirical evidence that practicing an "attitude of gratitude" works – it *does* make people happy.[28] I think this kind of research is interesting and important.

So, then, whose side am I on in the positive psychology wars? Treebeard says it best: "I am not altogether on anybody's side, because nobody is altogether on my side, if you understand me . . . There are some things, of course, whose side I am altogether not on; I am against them altogether."[29] Like Treebeard, I can tell you which sides I am altogether not on. I am not here to tell you that mindfulness doesn't work, that gratitude is a bust, that you should stop meditating or exercising or whatever else. If it works, don't stop. I know well that such things can be both metaphorical and literal life-savers.

But I'm also not here to tell you that you need to accept things the way they are, or to say *thank you*, or to smile.

The large-scale moral I want to draw from this part of the discussion is not that positive psychology is a good thing or a bad thing, but that the very fact that we place happiness in the domain of positive psychology entails that we are thinking of happiness as *a state of mind*. The old etymological connections with fate, circumstances or luck – "hap" in the original sense – have disappeared, and they have been replaced with this modern conception of happiness as a *nice feeling* or a *positive emotion*.

From a certain angle, this new conception of happiness looks pleasantly tame, where the old conception of "hap" was anything but. The role of fate or chance in the universe, and in our own existence, can make us feel quite powerless. Indeed, such thoughts can be existentially terrifying.

On the other hand, there is something deeply, existentially comforting about the idea that we *are* in control of our own individual circumstances. That "we make our own luck" – whether that means pulling ourselves up by our emotional or economic bootstraps or manifesting whatever we desire through positive thinking and wishing on stars.

But sometimes the scary thing is the truth. I think we need to recenter the role of luck and circumstance in the good life, as a corrective to the wildly popular Emotional Dream. The Dream *programs* us to engage in the pursuit of happiness, telling us it's our own responsibility to succeed, and then the Paradox of Happiness ensures that we hit a brick wall when we try.

Unfortunately, I don't think we can solve the Paradox just by reviewing the old solutions. Frankl and Mill and Sidgwick (and many, many others) have had important things to contribute, but they weren't facing the same incarnation of the problem that we're facing now. Frankl was perhaps the closest, especially in his observations about the injunction to "be happy" as characteristically American. But *we* face a world shaped by the mass global export of that ideology, and indeed a world that is being dominated and slowly consumed by the monster it has evolved into – Disney songs, *The Secret*, toxic positivity, alternative facts, Emotional Dream and all.

Even worse, I don't think the Paradox of Happiness is *just* a problem about happiness. If all this is true when it comes to happiness, it's true in spades when it comes to romantic love. If the pursuit of happiness is self-defeating, the pursuit of *happy ever after* should be at least equally doomed, and probably more so.

Perhaps, then, it's not surprising that so many of us run ourselves ragged in lifelong efforts to turn unhappy relation-ships into happy ones or run from unhappy relationships in hopes that the *next* one will supply the happy ever after that we seek. We're socially programmed to do this, just as we are to pursue happiness in general, with the weight of responsibility on us to succeed in the search. And, in that way, we are sent scurrying towards some very spiky and unpleasant dead ends.

That is the mechanism I'll try to lay bare over the course the next chapter.

2

# The Romantic Paradox

### Dreamlover

since feeling is first
who pays any attention
to the syntax of things
will never wholly kiss you;

wholly to be a fool
while Spring is in the world

my blood approves,
and kisses are a better fate
than wisdom
lady i swear by all flowers. Don't cry
– the best gesture of my brain is less than
your eyelids' flutter which says

we are for each other: then
laugh, leaning back in my arms
for life's not a paragraph
And death i think is no parenthesis

I discovered this famous poem by e e cummings when I was in
my late teens – a popular life phase for being "romantic" –
and I was bowled over by its beauty and power. I even put
parts of it in my email signature, which, let me tell you, was a
big deal at the time: this was back in the days when email was
a futuristic novelty, and it felt *self-defining* to include a quote
in one's email signature. That's how much I loved this poem.

Sadly, like all faves, it turned out to be pretty problematic.[1] There's lots to say about why. The comparison in the third stanza, for example, between "my brain" and "your eyelids' flutter" is calling attention to a stereotypically gendered selection of attributes: men have brains, women have fluttery eyelids. The poem does go on to say the male brain's "best gesture" is somehow "less than" the female eyelid flutter. But we're not fooled. That's not a sweet compliment – it's what's known in the trade as *benevolent sexism*.[2]

But it's actually another thread in the poem, something a bit subtler and more insidious, that I want to expand upon. I think doing so will help me put the Emotional Dream of chapter 1 in context and better explain the contemporary associations between happiness and love.

Taken as a whole, the poem is cautioning a "lady" against romancing anyone who thinks too much about the nitty-gritty details of life (the "syntax of life"). Instead, it recommends that she should be "a fool." The lady is told to laugh (ah, the long history of men telling women to smile) and lean back in the speaker's arms. She should surrender to feelings and not worry her pretty head with thoughts. She should choose "kisses" over "wisdom." This is all summed up tidily in the poem's very first line: "feeling is first." A perfect mission statement for romanticism. cummings's poem is a perfect snapshot of the romantic conception of love.[3] On this conception, love is identified with passion and emotion. It's a "feeling."

The poem was published in 1926, and the ideas about love and romance that it so beautifully and efficiently encapsulates were not plucked out of thin air. They were culturally ascendant at the time. This ascendancy of feeling is associated with Romanticism, an artistic and cultural movement occupying roughly the first half of the nineteenth century (the name of which is not, of course, a coincidence). While the appeal of Romanticism subsequently waned in many artistic contexts, romantic ideas about the nature of love became culturally dominant and remain so today.

Feeling is positioned by Romanticism as antithetical to thinking or rationality, as if there is antagonism and competition between feeling and thinking. Crucially, Romanticism also positions feeling as *first* in the sense that it's more important, more natural, more powerful, and just generally *better* than thinking.

Some of these romantic ideas about love and feeling were around before the twentieth century. But they weren't so common, even in poetic contexts. If one looks back to Shakespeare's love poems, for example, one finds far more emphasis on the physical beauty of the beloved. Many of the sonnets consist entirely in attempts to persuade the beloved to have children now so that her beauty can be reproduced in the next generation, or because she'll be old and ugly soon (neither of which strike me as *romantic* ways to persuade someone to go to bed with you).

At first, Romanticism was rather a radical idea – a reaction to the rationalism of the Enlightenment and to the prosaic, mechanistic world-view of the Industrial Revolution. The romantic emphasis on feelings suited nineteenth-century artists, rebels and other assorted "Bohemians." But it didn't become part of the expected, normal course of a human life until a century or so later.

If feeling takes priority over wisdom, that means there is some sort of choice to be made between them. They're in competition with each other. Setting aside the beauty of cummings's poetry and the depressing inevitability of his sexism, I want to examine his poem's romantic ideological core directly. *Is feeling first?*

If we buy into the received wisdom, we have to say "yes." The very things that define a good life are feelings:

1 A good life is one full of love and happiness. A bad life is one with neither.

Happiness (on the modern, tame, conception) is a nice feeling. And love, as I'll be arguing in this chapter, has come to be thought of as *another nice feeling*. That's why we talk about being in love as "having feelings" for someone or falling in love as "catching feelings."

I suggested in chapter 1 that American Dreams, including the Emotional Dream, have more or less programmed us to believe that wishing on stars is the solution to all our problems. What do we wish for? Some of us might wish for money. Living under capitalism, wishing for money is often simply wishing for survival. But the people wishing for money are misguided, according to the received wisdom. Remember the second and third messages:

2  Love and happiness (the best things in life) are "free."
3  In order to live a good life, one should *pursue* love and happiness (as opposed to crass things such as wealth, power or fame).

By these lights, if we want a good life, we should really be wishing for love and happiness, not money.

Many people do wish for love. And what they are specifically wishing for – the *kind* of love they have in mind – is often romantic love. The kind that comes with happiness (ever after) attached. That is the romantic dream. For the clearest prototypes of how this dream looks, we can go back again to Disney, this time to the 1959 film *Sleeping Beauty*. "I know you," sings the Prince on meeting Beauty for the first time, "I walked with you once upon a dream." And Beauty for her part sings that "Some day [her] prince will come . . . and away to his castle [they'll] go, to be happy forever."

The recipe for attaining this romantic dream is pretty clear in Disney, too: a rich man and a beautiful woman just have to stumble across each other by accident, fall passionately for each other at first sight, then, after some trials (which they eventually overcome) they will experience permanent happiness together. (As an aside: the need for the *beginning* of one's love story to resemble this paradigm accounts for the hesitancy that many once felt – and some still feel – around admitting that they met their life partners through dating agencies or other precursors of online dating. "Willing to lie about how we met" used to be a common line in dating ads.[4] Nowadays the prevalence of online dating has to some extent normalized the idea that meeting someone isn't a random accident, with interesting consequences which I'll discuss further later in this book.)

Perhaps you aren't convinced of the relevance of a 1950s cartoon song to contemporary romance (though remember things such as this deeply influenced millions of us in early childhood, long before we were old enough to engage our critical thinking defenses). If so, how about Mariah Carey's 1993 hit "Dreamlover," in which she expresses basically the same ideas as Beauty, only with a touch less patience? "Dreamlover come rescue me, / Take me up take me down, / Take me anywhere you want to baby now. I need you so desperately, / Won't you please come around, /'Cause I wanna share forever with you baby." It's not about any one song. It's about how everyone is singing the same tune everywhere we look.

And it's the fact that everyone is telling the same one story. There's a reason we can all cite the same plot formula of a romance: "boy meets girl, boy loses girl, boy gets girl back again." Contemporary romcoms proceed from a cute initial meeting, through a series of apparently insuperable obstacles, to a surprise resolution that brings about the desired "happy ending" for the couple.

Our romantic script is very simple and has been pretty consistent over the course of the last century or century and a half. Its central features are initial sexual attraction (heterosexual by default) leading to intimate loving connection and monogamous marriage (or marriage-like status), followed by biological reproduction and the formation of a nuclear family. There are a whole bunch of problematic gender norms bundled up with each step.[5] But, most importantly for current purposes, this is what's being presented to us in our songs and stories as the path to "happy ever after."

Such focused story-telling yields a weird mixture of an offer and a threat: "You want to be happy for ever, don't you? Well then, you'd better follow this script!"

### They can't really be happy

Like most of us, when I started to fall in love with people and enter into relationships, I tried to follow the script. I started monogamous, committed heterosexual relationships and I tried to get my happy ever after from them.

I had never seen or heard a story about a non-monogamous relationship until I was in my thirties. Or, more accurately, I had never until then seen or heard a story about a non-monogamous relationship *that wasn't a disaster*. I did encounter stories from time to time – in gossip about other people's break-ups or sub-plots on sitcoms – that made plain to me that non-monogamy was at best a joke and at worst a life-wreckingly stupid idea. The people in these stories were not role models. They were creepy, immoral, deceptive, explosive, abusive, or just plain *bad*. So non-monogamy wasn't a live option on my roadmap for life. (Until I was in my twenties, bisexuality wasn't a live option either.)

Anyone *can*, of course, choose not to follow the scripted path to happy ever after. We *can* bravely cast out into our own uncharted territories. But a very important fact about doing that is it makes us into *rebels*, with all that that entails. Doing something in a context where it's rebellious, or contrary to one's cultural script, is not the same thing as doing it in a neutral context. (Consider the difference between being a woman who doesn't shave her armpits and being a man who doesn't shave his armpits.)

Now, in my forties, I have some experience of being a rebel when it comes to romance. Being polyamorous means that I do not fit my assigned role in the romantic script, because I don't stick to the monogamy norm. But I don't *like* being a rebel. I'm the kind of person who avoids conflict like a plague. I was a good kid all through school. I worked hard, got excellent grades, and never wanted any trouble from authority figures. Once, a teacher separated me from my friend because we were giggling in class. I never got over it. I cry for days when people are mean to me. I obey traffic laws even if nobody is watching.

When I started living openly as polyamorous, all the stories I'd heard about non-monogamy, all the vague warnings and threats, started to become self-fulfilling prophecies. As I mentioned in my preface, when I started talking about polyamory on a public stage I got so much horrible feedback that I became depressed. I'm not cut out to be a rebel. I'd describe myself more as a people-pleaser who gets hate mail. But this is how social policing works to keep rebels in line.

And not all of it is vicious or unkindly meant. Some people were concerned for me precisely because, like me until I was thirty, they had only heard disastrous stories about non-monogamy. So they thought I was headed for disaster, and they tried to ward me away from it. Back to the safe path, the happy ever after trajectory. But intentions are irrelevant. The effects were that people I cared deeply about started saying awful, unkind things about my relationships. I lost some friends. It hurt. (It was interesting to see, though, that here, too, people would talk about whether or not my relationships were "happy" as if that were equivalent to an assessment of whether they were any *good*.)

Lack of social support disproportionately impacts stigmatized or marginalized relationships. This is perhaps obvious enough, but it is also supported by a body of research. For example, in a 2006 study,[6] psychologists report finding that "individuals who perceived greater disapproval of their relationships had significantly lower levels of commitment, suggesting that perceptions of marginalization may indeed affect how people feel about their partners." More recently, a 2015 paper[7] reports on multiple studies finding "extensive support for the social network effect, whereby relationship approval from family and friends leads individuals to feel more love, more committed, and more positive about a partner." Now consider who is more likely to have their friends and relations whispering behind their back that they "can't really be happy" in their current relationship: Simone, who's in a polyamorous relationship with a trans woman, or Sarah, who's monogamously married to a cis hetero man?

I've heard more times than I care to remember that I can't possibly be happy with my husband, since we are not monogamous. I've been strongly advised against "that" kind of relationship, both by random internet jerks and by some of my nearest and dearest. I suppose my marriage must be a pretty strong one to have withstood such a barrage of attempts to undermine it and convince me that it's never going to work.

Another way people police relationship structures is to *erase* certain stories: just pretend they don't exist. This kind of erasure does not have to be done deliberately or maliciously to have the effect. Again, intentions are irrelevant. What matters is the result.

Here's an example of the kind of thing I mean. In 2017, black polyamorous author and blogger Kevin Patterson and his wife Antoinette Patterson were interviewed for a high-profile *New York Times* article on open relationships. There was a photoshoot of the two of them. But the picture chosen to appear with the article and the way their stories were used in the piece itself were deeply troubling to Kevin Patterson. He says of the experience:

> I'm not flat out saying that my wife and I are only included as token people of color. I am challenging anyone to show

me what the difference would be if we were. Our voices are mostly unused, but our faces are pretty prominent in a photo that shocked the people in our lives. One friend said it is the *saddest they've ever seen either of us look*.[8]

Here he's describing how the casual racism of using black people's images in a tokenistic way, while excluding their voices, intersected with the *erasure of happiness* from his non-monogamous love story. For what it's worth, I've seen the photo of the Pattersons that appeared in the *NYT* article, and I think it looks like a photo of a cheating husband seeking forgiveness from a long-suffering wife. It's incredibly misleading.

As Patterson goes on to explain, the *NYT* article centers the narrative of a married couple who turn to non-monogamy as a band-aid solution to address their failing relationship. This is one of those sad cultural stereotypes I had heard all about in my formative years – indeed, it's one of those stereotypes we *all* hear about quite often. It's hardly *NYT*-worthy news. As Patterson puts it: "[T]he idea that ethical and consensual non-monogamy are just the product of unhappy marriages is already the predominant narrative. We've heard these stories before. They get pushed out to mainstream media every few months and frankly it's gotten boring."

But it wasn't that the journalist had only sad stories to tell. Patterson and his wife had handed her a different story, as well as a different image. Their happiness was simply erased from the published copy. That is how popular mainstream media serves to reinforce existing scripts, including the stereotype that no one can "really be happy" in a non-monogamous relationship.

And it works. When *What Love Is* came out, I did quite a few talks and interviews, and, over time, I started to notice some patterns in the questions that kept coming up. One was that people seemed to be very keen on getting me to talk more about "the downsides" of polyamory. It eventually became evident that, when reading my book or coming to hear me talk about it, they expected misery. They wanted a least a *little* bit of misery, or they felt sort of cheated. As if I was telling the story wrong. Polyamory isn't supposed to be a happy ever after story.

For the most part, they specifically wanted me to talk about the painful and destructive effects of jealousy in non-monogamous relationships. I hadn't said much about jealousy in my book, besides making a few remarks of a theoretical nature, because it hadn't been a big part of my own experience of non-monogamy. (It *had*, for what it's worth, once or twice been an upsetting part of my experience of monogamy, but that didn't seem particularly relevant for the book and probably wasn't what this segment of my audience was looking for either!) In the end, I developed a kind of "standard response package" for these folks, the bulk of which consisted of my explaining how, if jealousy *were* a big problem for me, I would be trying a different approach to my relationships.

What was interesting about all this to me, though, was not just that so many people expected to hear about polyamory's "downsides." It was the fact that they *thought they knew what those would be*. I suppose wanting to hear about the downsides could be driven by any number of conscious or unconscious motives – anything from an uneasy desire to be reassured that one isn't really missing out on a good thing to a generic fascination with someone else's train wreck. But this uniform ability to fill in the details of what those downsides ought to look like – that is a testament to the power of stories. The power of the stories we tell over and over and the power of the stories we never hear.

In any case, the misery-laden stereotype of non-monogamy remains live. It serves as a warning to others: a cautionary tale to keep them in line. (Don't go *that* way, or you'll be sorry!)

One way we keep it alive is by erasing the stories of happy polyamorous people. Another is by *discounting* such stories if we do happen to come across one: distrusting or denying what happy polyamorous people have to say about their own experiences, for example. This second mechanism is part of a more general phenomenon that feminist philosophers call "testimonial injustice."[9] It happens when certain groups of people are discredited, even if they have relevant knowledge or expertise, because of systemic prejudice against those groups. Women, for example, are routinely subject to testimonial injustice when they are disbelieved or ignored regarding their experiences of sexual assault.[10] Similarly, polyamorous people are subject to testimonial injustice when they are disbelieved or ignored regarding their experiences of happy non-monogamous love.

But surely, you might hope, we would listen if some real *experts* told us about whether polyamorous people are happy? If by "experts" you mean *scientists*, then unfortunately the answer is probably still "no." Recently, a team of psychologists found that researchers are perceived as being *more biased* when presenting data that favours polyamory than when presenting data that favours monogamy.[11] It's as if the world doesn't want to hear anything good about non-monogamous relationships. You try to tell such a story, and they put their hands over their ears and yell "La la la," until you give up.

I'm just using non-monogamous love as an example here. It's relatively easy for me to talk about this because I have some experience of it. (And obviously I also have a vested interest in getting more philosophical discussion of polyamory on the agenda.) But essentially the same pattern shows up with any kind of non-conforming relationship. The *happy* stories about non-conforming love are for the most part never told. And, even when they are told, in one way or another we refuse to hear them. This is especially true of stories where women eschew romantic love altogether in favour of loving friendships, family or community. (Where are the happy spinsters to balance out the Miss Havishams and the Miss Gulches and the Lily Barts and the Sister Carries?)[12]

The message is loud and clear: don't have *too many* romantic partners, and don't have *too few* either. One dreamlover each.

## Mad love

While being left a spinster may be a bad ending for women in fiction, it's usually a cold, slow, *dull* bad ending, whereas sad love – the dramatic, tragic kind of sad love we know from all the operas and pop songs – is the plot equivalent of a Vesuvian eruption. It's instantly disastrous and, honestly, you're lucky if you survive at all.

These images of sad love play into the idea of love being all about feelings, as I mentioned earlier. There's something else going on here, too: they present love as something that is completely out of our control. Something like an addiction, as popular scientist of love Helen Fisher argues.[13] Or perhaps a form of madness. Romanticism in general pits feeling against thinking, emotion against rationality. Seeing love as a kind of addiction or madness is one instance of this general pattern.

I mentioned earlier that some of the core ideas of Romanticism were around before the nineteenth century, although they were less culturally dominant during the Enlightenment and Renaissance eras. If we go back all the way to ancient Greece and Rome, however, we can pull out a strand of thought that is important for how we think about love today.

"Eros" is an ancient Greek word translated variously as *love*, *passion* or *erotic desire*. (It's also the name of the god who is a personification of these things and the etymological ancestor of our word *erotic*.) Contemporary classicist (and poet) Anne Carson gives us an illuminating explanation of eros in her 1989 book *Eros the Bittersweet*. She argues, drawing in a huge range of literature (from Sappho and Homer to Rilke and Emily Dickinson), that eros has been conceived in much the same way from ancient Greece to the present day.

This version of eros is essentially bittersweet (both painful and pleasurable), and as such it is paradoxical or self-contradictory in nature. Carson also explains that eros consists in a state of lack or need, a kind of desperate grasping for the "beloved," and that it can never be fully satisfied (or else it is extinguished and ceases to exist). Eros is thus unstable by nature.

This picture of eros fits neatly with the idea that people in love are irrational, or even crazy. Who can make rational sense of a thing that contradicts itself? It's an impossible task! Love is crazy-making. Feelings don't make any sense and can't be controlled. All of this feeds into what I've called the Romantic Mystique,[14] a piece of romantic ideology that tells us love is an ineffable mystery, in the face of which we do best simply to surrender like the "fool" of cummings's poem. We shouldn't try to understand. Shouldn't try to educate ourselves.

Why would we disempower ourselves like this? What do we gain from reveling in our own ignorance when it comes to love? One classic approach to criminal investigation is to ask *cui bono* (or, in English, *who benefits*). The Romantic Mystique serves to protect love from examination and critique: if we believe we'll never be able to control love or even understand it, we're more willing to acquiesce to the harms done in its name. By stifling understanding and criticism, the Romantic Mystique hinders change and progress. It protects the status quo, and as such it serves the interests of whomever benefits from the status quo: those who are privileged within the "traditional" nuclear family structure. That arrangement developed under patriarchy to position (straight, cis) men as the heads of households. Seen in this light, poetically advising a woman to "be a fool" and "laugh" about surrendering to romance strikes a much darker note.

Certainly people experience powerful emotions, driven by the ancient biological machinery that we are made of. These experiences *can* make us feel crazy or make us behave like addicts. The question is what to call them. Under the sway of romantic ideology, we call them "love." Under the conception of love I'll develop throughout this book, I doubt they would count. We could call them infatuation, or romantic obsession, or "limerence" – a word coined by Dorothy Tennov in 1979 to capture an involuntary state involving obsessive and intrusive thinking and extremes of positive and negative emotion.[15]

It's important not to imagine that limerence is a kind of love. Entering the state is often called "falling in love" – by scientists and philosophers as well as in everyday conversation – but this is a mistake. You can experience limerence for someone you don't know well (or at all), or even for someone you dislike. When pressed on the question, most of us will acknowledge that you can't *really* be "in love" in these situations. We make distinctions by saying it's "just a crush," not "the real thing."

This isn't just a verbal disagreement about how to use the word "love." It's also about getting our concepts straight, which means it is about how we think. And how we think impacts everything we do. Confusing limerence with love is a mistake that can have serious consequences. Love is positioned as one of the best things in life and (alongside happiness) one of the twin goals of a good life. We are programmed to sacrifice more or less everything for love. The involuntary and irrational state of limerence is a terrible candidate to play such a role.

We're all familiar with the stereotype of foolish teenagers acting wildly under the influence of crushes while the old folks look wisely on and scoff at their immaturity. The clash between Romanticism's "feeling is first" ideology and a sensible but dull and "unromantic" approach to life is often dramatized as a clash between youth and age. But it's *not* just foolish teenagers who mistake limerence for love.

The unstable and contradictory eros (which Anne Carson so beautifully describes in *Eros the Bittersweet*) is often called "love" by Carson herself, as well as by many of the poets and authors she discusses. Scientists, too, will often describe themselves as studying "love" or "romantic love," then proceed to investigate something that looks much more like limerence. The so-called Passionate Love Scale, one of the most commonly used tools in this area of psychological literature, begins by asking subjects how much they agree with the following statements:

1 Since I've been involved with _____, my emotions have been on a roller coaster.
2 I would feel deep despair if _____ left me.
3 Sometimes my body trembles with excitement at the sight of _____.
4 I take delight in studying the movements and angles of _____'s body.
5 Sometimes I feel I can't control my thoughts; they are obsessively on _____.

These all sound like symptoms of limerence and/or eros: something obsessive, turbulent, overwrought, out of control.[16] A kind of madness. But, on the romantic conception, that's what love is. One contemporary philosopher of love, Arina Pismenny, captures this neatly: "Romantic love is an obsessive passionate state characterized by intense and varied emotional experiences, intrusive thinking, and idealization of the beloved, who occupies center stage in one's mind."[17]

Obsession, intrusive thoughts, and excesses of intense emotion are symptomatic of a number of mental disorders. The history of thinking of love as a (mental or physical) "sickness" is long and colourful.[18] But our current way of thinking about it is perhaps best summarized by love scientist Helen Fisher: "men and women who are passionately in love and/or rejected in love show the basic symptoms of substance-related and gambling addiction listed in the Diagnostic and Statistical Manual of Mental Disorders-5, including craving, mood modification, tolerance, emotional and physical dependence and withdrawal."[19]

## The pursuit of happy ever after

Remember the Paradox of Happiness from chapter 1? Pursuing happiness doesn't work and actually tends to make us unhappy. I think there is an exactly analogous problem with romantic love, and I'm going to round out this chapter by expanding on that thought.

I'm not going to call this new paradox the "Paradox of Love," though. This paradox doesn't have a name already, so I get to name it myself, and I want a name that makes it clear exactly where the blame lies. So I'm not calling this the "Paradox of Love" because, in my opinion, love is not the problem – at least not on the eudaimonic conception of love that I will be developing here. The problem is our romantic ideology of love. So I'm calling this the Romantic Paradox.

The Romantic Paradox is simply this: chasing the romantic "happy ever after" tends to make us unhappy. It's the special case of the Paradox of Happiness that you get by restricting attention to a particular kind of happiness, namely the kind alluded to in the romantic "happy ever after." We could phrase a version of the Romantic Paradox by analogy with Mill's version of the Paradox of Happiness: "those only are happy ever after who have their minds fixed on some object other than their own happiness ever after." Or we could phrase a version by analogy with Frankl: "happiness ever after cannot be pursued; it must ensue."

The Romantic Paradox is not guaranteed to be a genuine problem just because the original Paradox of Happiness is one. Maybe pursuing happiness in general tends to make us unhappy, but pursuing this kind of happiness is just fine. By analogy, reading online comments in general tends to make me feel bad, but reading online comments on cute photos of labradoodles tends to be pretty OK. So why believe the Romantic Paradox is really a paradox?

We saw in chapter 1 how much of the Paradox of Happiness is bound up with construal of happiness as akin to pleasure a nice feeling, or a "positive emotion".[20] Part of why I think the two will pattern similarly is that love is also often positioned as a "positive emotion" under the romantic conception. One exponent of this idea is Barbara Fredrickson, a prominent contemporary researcher in the field of positive psychology. Fredrickson is concerned with the question of why, from an evolutionary perspective, we would have positive emotions. You can see why a "negative" (i.e. unpleasant) emotion such as fear could be useful: it's a good idea to be afraid of tigers so that you run away from them and they don't eat you. But what survival value do positive (pleasant) emotions have?

Fredrickson's answer consists in her highly influential "broaden-and-build" theory.[21] As she summarizes it: "positive emotions serve to broaden an individual's momentary thought-action repertoire, which in turn has the effect of building that individual's physical, intellectual, and social resources." In effect, the suggestion here is that positive emotions are useful because they enable us to pay attention to more than just our most immediate needs and dangers. While negative emotions tend to narrow our focus – fear, for example, concentrates the mind on the approaching tiger – positive ones tend to *broaden* our attention to the people and environment around us. When we enjoy a landscape, we can spend time surveying its large-scale composition and its specific features. When we enjoy someone's company, we want to learn more about them, and we take time to notice things we otherwise wouldn't. This helps to *build* and strengthen both our social bonds and our understanding of the world. In general, feeling good tends to make us more expansive and more open to learning a wide range of new kinds of information.

That all sounds quite convincing to me. But what grabs my attention most in Fredrickson's classic paper is the fact that her list of positive emotions – the ones she places at the center of her discussion – consists of "joy, interest, contentment, and love."[22] She mentions that love may take a variety of different forms, but romantic love is explicitly included in her discussion. Fredrickson also makes clear that what distinguishes the positive emotions is that they "share a pleasant subjective feel."

Like e e cummings, Fredrickson isn't pulling this idea from nowhere. She's not being at all *idiosyncratic* in classifying love as a positive emotion or a nice feeling. Doing so is entirely in keeping with contemporary psychology at large and with the broader cultural context that shapes and structures its subject matter (that is, our minds). Psychology doesn't operate in a vacuum: it's just another mirror, here reflecting back to us something about our dominant conception of what love is.

Of course, love on the romantic conception is often said to include *nasty* feelings, as well as nice feelings – that's why eros is called "bittersweet," after all. But insofar as we set ourselves in pursuit of romantic "happy ever afters," we are presumably chasing the sweet part – the positive emotion – not the bitter part. And, more importantly, whether nice or nasty, love on the dominant romantic conception is all about feelings. Just as with happiness, when love is reduced to feelings it loses its connections to things that are bigger than individuals. But I'll say more about that in the next chapter.

Nothing here looks as if it will dissolve the Romantic Paradox by showing it to be disanalogous with the Paradox of Happiness. If anything, the pursuit of happy ever after may be even *likelier* to be self-defeating. For one thing, romantic happiness is accorded a special place in our social structure, positioned as the highest and best kind of happiness. So the stakes are higher and our investment more intense. (This also explains the association with plunging straight into the depths of despair when things go wrong – the tragic version of sad love I described in the introduction is simply the flip side of this way of thinking.) For another, our cultural image of "eros" is, by its very nature, something that *can't be satisfied* – if we achieve the object of our eros then eros dies.

And there's another problem too: it's not just the "happy" part that we're pursuing. The "ever after" part is also liable to create problems of its own. The romantic ideal is an image of *static* love: "happy ever after" comes at the end of the story because, once it arrives, there's nothing else to tell. Nothing ever changes.

Here is a passage from one of Shakespeare's most popular sonnets, Sonnet CXVI, beautifully expounding this static conception of love:

> Love is not love
> Which alters when it alteration finds,
> Or bends with the remover to remove:
> O, no! it is an ever-fixed mark,
> That looks on tempests and is never shaken . . .

Now this is one Shakespeare sonnet that *does* sound romantic. That – I would hypothesize – is why it's so famous and why it's much more likely that you'd hear this sonnet quoted at a wedding today than Sonnet II (which is all about how you'll be ugly when you're forty and you'll be really sad about it unless you have some kids pronto). But this kind of fixed thinking can be quite damaging to relationships. A healthy relationship is something dynamic that grows and changes over time along with the people in it. When that stops happening, the creature is no longer alive. (I'll say more about this in later chapters.)

Nevertheless, the static picture is (still) all too often seen through rose-tinted specs, especially in connection with romantic ideas about being "fated" or "destined" to be with someone. People talk about meeting "the one," their "soul-mate," their "twin flame," their "perfect match" or their "other half." This may sound like a romantic dream, but there is some empirical research to suggest that this might, on the contrary, be *harming* our chances of finding romantic happiness.

In a 2014 paper,[23] psychologists Spike Lee and Norbert Schwarz point out that "[l]ove can be metaphorically framed as perfect unity between two halves made for each other," or as "a journey with ups and downs." They wanted to test whether these ways of thinking had differential impacts on relationship satisfaction, hypothesizing that "people may evaluate their relationship more negatively after thinking about relational conflicts in the unity frame (wherein con-flicts signal disunity) than in the journey frame (wherein conflicts are part of progress)." So they cued some of their participants with ideas about unity (using phrases such as "we were made for each other") and the rest with ideas about journey and progress (phrases such as "look how far we've come"). Then they asked participants to imagine relation-ship conflicts and evaluate how they felt about the relation-ship afterwards. They found that thinking about conflicts damaged relationship satisfaction *more* when participants were prompted to think about love as perfect unity (what I would call a static conception) than when they thought of it as a journey (a dynamic conception).

There are certainly other reasons to distrust the idea of a romantic partner being one's "other half," not least the fact that it encourages us to think of ourselves as being *incomplete* or *inadequate* without a partner. But for current purposes I mostly want to emphasize how this idea feeds into the Romantic Paradox: chasing after romantic union with "the one" tends to damage the very relationships that are supposed to deliver that blissful state.

Romantic love is like happiness: the more we chase after it, the more it eludes us. That's not surprising given that we define one in terms of the other.

But just how bad a problem is this? Are romantic love and happiness really the best things life has to offer?[24]

# 3

# Daimons

## The ghosts of old meanings

When you fall down the rabbit hole of trying to figure out what counts as a good life, you can start to feel like you're being haunted by some very old ghosts. The question is ancient, and some of the putative answers – including some that we still take seriously today – are thousands of years old. This means ancient ways of thinking about these subjects are still here, although their original contexts are long gone. These are like the disembodied souls of old systems of meaning: conceptual ghosts, rustling and whispering in the background of our thought processes.

If words are the pieces from which sentences are built, concepts are the pieces from which thoughts are built. We can think of a concept as what a word expresses – the idea behind the word. Concepts frame our whole experience of the world. They determine what we can and can't process, what we do and don't understand, what we can and cannot learn. They quietly structure everything.

One particular concept has been haunting me these last few years, and over time it's been clawing at my attention more and more. This is the concept of *eudaimonia*. It's an ancient piece of conceptual technology, one that's been deployed and refined over thousands of years by philosophers trying to understand what counts as living a good life.

By far the most famous theory of eudaimonia (by which most others are more or less directly influenced) comes from the Greek philosopher Aristotle, who lived in the fourth century BCE and theorized that a good life is a eudaimonic life. In modern English translations of Aristotle's writings, "eudaimonia" is sometimes translated as *happiness*. This is disputed, however, with others arguing that *well-being* or *flourishing* would be closer to what Aristotle had in mind. Given the contemporary understanding of happiness in terms of positive emotions or pleasurable feelings, the latter seems more accurate. Aristotle's eudaimonia is bound up with notions of virtue – to be eudaimonic, for Aristotle, meant you had to be a good person. He also says that what counts as eudaimonia is determined by your nature, which depends on your species. And, because humans are distinctively rational (so he says), human eudaimonia is about the proper deployment of our rationality. Aristotle also says some very unsettling things, such as that unattractive people can't fully achieve eudaimonia. There is some debate as to what he could have meant by that (beyond just "it sucks to be ugly").

In any case, this never sounded entirely promising to me. Aristotle's work and its philosophical descendants aren't the reason I'm interested in eudaimonia.[1] It's something else – something even older than Aristotle.

Because it's so old, the ghost concept *eudaimonia* appears to us in strange linguistic clothing. The Greek word was imported into English wholesale and hasn't undergone significant evolution during the intervening period. In that sense it's well preserved. We can see inside it and take a look at its internal components in some detail. The word "eudaimonia" is built from ancient Greek roots: "eu" – meaning *good*, the same meaning we also see preserved in words such as "euphoria" and "euphemism" – and "daimon," which means *divine entity* or *supernatural being* or *spirit*. So the original meaning of *eudaimonia* has something to do with *good spirits*.

But what exactly was a "daimon?" It could be any number of things. More or less any kind of supernatural or incorporeal being might have been called a daimon, depending on who you asked: anything from a full-on super-powerful deity, down through the ranks of demi-gods, right down to a personal guardian spirit, like a guardian angel. The modern English word "demon" is our only surviving direct etymological descendant of "daimon," but it can be a bit misleading to think of daimons as demons, since in the original Greek there was no connotation of evil.

A personal guardian daimon is comparable to what in ancient Rome would have been called a "genius." In fact, the Latin word "genius" is also glittering with etymological clues. Originally, it referred not to a clever or creative *person* but to the attendant spirit who watched over them and inspired their creations. A person's greatest accomplishments were, at one time, attributed to the aid of their personal daimon. The word "genius" shares the same root as "genetics" and "generation," because all of them have something to do with birth. Your genius was a spirit who'd be with you from the moment you were born, or even a little beforehand in some versions of the mythology.[2] At the end of Plato's *Republic*, for example, Socrates describes how, after death, souls that are due for another mortal life get to choose for themselves what kind of life it will be. And they choose a new genius (a daimon) to guide them through that process of reincarnation and then throughout their next life. A genius, so imagined, is a kind of shadowy entity, a constant presence in the background of your life. Because their job is to guide you to live your life as well as possible, your genius tries to nudge you towards those brilliant ideas that seem to come to you out of nowhere.

Over time, we decided it was more realistic to attribute all those brilliant ideas and inspired artworks to the individual – to the "great man" himself. And so the word "genius" came to refer to the great man, not to some ghostly entity giving him all the right nudges in the all the right directions. I'm not convinced that this newer vision of what's happening *is* more realistic: I'm more inclined to believe that we simply replaced one mythology with another and, in the process, have lost sight of something important. The place I feel this loss most is when it comes to interpreting "eudaimonia," this ancient word that once had something to do with good spirits – that is, good daimons.

Aristotle basically ignored this older meaning of "eudaimonia,"[3] but it can still be detected in etymological traces. And something has kept whispering in my ear that the old meaning – the *very* old meaning – of "eudaimonia" holds a clue about what it means to live a good life, a clue that went missing with Aristotle. Something like an old forgotten magic, with the power to free us from this spell we've fallen under: to release us from the *glamour*[4] of "happy ever after."

In its original sense, "eudaimonia" might mean something like being watched over by a good daimon. Or perhaps it might mean having a good working relationship with your daimon. If you were eudaimonic in this sense, your guardian daimon would have your back. They might be a somewhat lowly superbeing – no Zeus or Hera, sure – but they'd be nudging you in good directions. You could make a good team with your daimon, and that might make great things possible for you: maybe you'd spend your life enjoying wonderful poetry, or friends, or philosophy, or family. Or all of the above. Or something else awesome: basically, whatever it would take to make your life a good one. A eudaimonic one.

This is already quite intriguing to me. But once we're thinking of a good life in terms of good daimons, there are also some other fascinating avenues to explore. Eudaimonia could be the beneficial impact of your own personal daimon, but it could also be that of a much larger, more powerful supernatural entity. For any kind of thing that could once have been called a "daimon," there are good and bad ways it might affect you, and the good ways are kinds of eudaimonia.

So another kind of eudaimonia comes with being favoured by very powerful beings, of the kind the ancient Greeks would have thought of as gods or demi-gods. This connects the ancient Greek word "daimon" back to its even older, proto-Indo-European root "deh-," which means *to give* or *distribute*. Daimons were originally so called because they were responsible for distributing fate. A daimon was a dispenser of destiny. If some really top-tier daimons are looking out for you, your life will be extremely fortunate. You'll be "hap"py in the old-fashioned sense of fortunate – your hap being a matter of what you were handed by the various invisible but powerful forces surrounding you.

These two very old ideas, ghosts of the old meaning of "eudaimonia," have now become two pillars of my contemporary theory of eudaimonia, or what it means to live a good life. First: your eudaimonia is about collaborations that make wonderful, meaningful pursuits possible for you. Second: your eudaimonia is shaped by a multiplicity of forces that surround you and shape your destiny.

I don't mean that we need to believe in literal spirits following us around in order to understand what it means to live a good life. A metaphorical understanding will do just as well. We often call someone our "fairy godmother" or "guardian angel" in metaphorical ways. Or we might talk, a bit more abstractly, about the "good vibe" in a place or the "positive spirit" of a work environment. We know what that kind of language means, even if we don't literally believe in fairies, angels, vibes or spirits. Daimons of the more abstract kind – atmospheres, Zeitgeists, and the like – come in different scales or sizes, from small and local to grand and sweeping. We could talk about the daimon of a work meeting we attended last Tuesday (small and localized), or that of Mozart's Vienna (somewhat larger), or that of the patriarchy (relatively huge).

Some thinkers posit literal daimons at every scale of reality, insofar as they believe that every organized or structured system has some sort of consciousness or mind. This is a variant of the view known as *panpsychism* (from the ancient Greek words "pan" – all, everything – and "psyche" – soul, breath, spirit). Versions of panpsychist thought have appeared in various philosophical, spiritual, religious and magical traditions. And, from a scientific perspective, panpsychism is sometimes put forward as a putative explanation of why we (humans) are conscious. Contemporary philosopher David Chalmers explores it in this light – his TED talk "How do you explain consciousness?" offers an accessible introduction to panpsychism (especially useful for those for whom the entire idea sounds too bizarre or too spooky to be taken seriously). One thesis that Chalmers (like others of a similarly scientific bent) finds worth exploring is that consciousness is a universal and fundamental property of physical systems, comparable to other, more familiar, fundamental properties such as mass and electric charge.[5]

Treating all daimons as literal minds or consciousnesses is more than I'm signing up for in this book. It's the metaphor of daimons that interests me. But it's worth noticing that, even if we did think of daimons as quite literally conscious spirits, that would not rule out the possibility that there are daimons, of many different sizes and degrees of complexity, everywhere we look.

My idea is that you can frame thoughts about what a good life would be like by imagining your life going *as if* there were good daimons all around you. In my own life, I hope for the kind of connections, environment and support systems that function like benevolent daimons: good spirits who can inspire me to make sound decisions and pursue my meaningful projects, and kind gods who can put the conditions in place to make my creative life possible.

## Eudaimonia vs. the Paradox of Happiness

A paradox is like a geode: a sparkly interior, encrusted with a rough and misleading shell. The Paradox of Happiness conceals, at its crystalline center, something of value that is worth seeing. But cracking a paradox open is work. It makes demands of us.

Let's look at J. S. Mill's statement of the Paradox of Happiness one more time:

> Those only are happy ... who have their minds fixed on some object other than their own happiness; on the happiness of others, on the improvement of mankind, even on some art or pursuit, followed not as a means, but as itself an ideal end. Aiming thus at something else, they find happiness by the way.

This statement could be helpfully clarified by replacing "happiness" with "hedonic happiness." As I mentioned in the last chapter, "hedone" is the Greek word for pleasure or nice feelings, and happiness, as it's typically understood nowadays, is hedonic happiness. We positioned romantic love, similarly, as being all about feelings. In the bad case, it is a dramatic, tragic state of madness or misery. But, in the good case, it is associated with intense (hedonic) happiness.

The moral of the paradox, for Mill, is that we need to aim at "something else," and hedonic happiness will come as a side effect. We might jump on that idea to claim that eudaimonia is the "something else" that solves the Paradox of Happiness. After all, eudaimonia is not hedonic happiness: it's not even about feelings.[6] But the solution can't be as simple as saying that, instead of pursuing happiness, we should pursue eudaimonia instead. That kind of quick response ignores all the real work.

It ignores, in particular, the social, cultural and political context that sets us up to be trapped by the paradox. Understanding how that context sets us up for the kind of failure the paradox describes is crucial if we are to uncover what's really at the heart of it. This is why I spent time on those "received wisdoms" from the introduction and on the American Dreams of chapter 1. Among other things, this work can lead us to question whether living a good life is really about "pursuing" or "aiming at" (or even attaining) anything. But, more generally, and most importantly, it must be taken into consideration in order to articulate what a proper concept of eudaimonia *is*.

I emphasize what it *is*, not what it *was* (for Aristotle, or for J. S. Mill, or for Viktor Frankl, or any of the other past thinkers we're discussing). *Our* proper concept of eudaimonia must be one that works in our circumstances, our social and cultural contexts, our lives. In fact, I might need to drop the "our" here to be really clear: the concept of eudaimonia *I* am looking for is one that fits *my* specific context. To the extent that your situation is similar to mine, what I find might be useful to you, but eudaimonia is going to turn out to be quite a complex and customizable thing.

Still, as always, we can gather clues from what others have suggested. Mill offered a few ideas about what kind of "something else" he thinks we are supposed to aim at. It's not just any old thing: "the happiness of others . . . the improvement of mankind, even . . . some art or pursuit." Why these, we might ask? What do they have in common? What makes *them* the right kinds of "something else?"

Viktor Frankl, whom we met briefly in chapter 1, encourages us to orient our lives towards something meaningful to us, rather than pursuing happiness. Having a reason to live, he says, amounts to finding meaning or purpose in one's life, and that is much more fundamental than happiness. Frankl's experience of serving as a therapist to suicidal prisoners in a World War II concentration camp led him to the conclusion that it was not happiness but meaning that made the difference between survival and despair. Frankl came to describe his mode of psychiatric treatment as *logotherapy*, from "logos," an ancient Greek word that can be translated as *word*, *plan* or *reason*. (It's also the root of our word "logic.") He postulated that human beings have a "will to meaning:"[7] a deep-seated drive or desire to find meaning in life.

By using this particular phrasing, Frankl is intentionally comparing his view with that of Friedrich Nietzsche.
Nietzsche, who had a rather different take on what makes
humanity tick, talked about the "will to power" as our most
basic driving force. Nietzsche's writings about power are
inconsistent and unclear, but one relatively clear statement,
from his 1886 book *Beyond Good and Evil*, is that "[a] living
thing seeks above all to DISCHARGE its strength – life itself
is WILL TO POWER." While Nietzsche actually agreed with
Frankl (and so many others) that it is meaning, not happiness, that should direct our lives, he seems to have had his
own definite ideas about what *makes* a life meaningful, as a
result of which he gives power the more fundamental role in
his philosophy.

Frankl also discusses Sigmund Freud, who puts neither
meaning nor power but *pleasure* in the driver's seat. Freud's
"pleasure principle"[8] can be interpreted as the thesis that
humans have a powerful and deep-rooted "will to pleasure,"
and that this guides their actions and shapes their lives.
Famously, Freud also assumes that the relevant kind of
pleasure is most often sexual in nature.

Do we humans truly have a basic will to meaning? Or to
power, or to pleasure? To something else altogether? I don't
claim to know the answer to that question. In fact, I am
suspicious that there could ever *be* a singular answer that
applied to everyone. Be that as it may, I feel as if Frankl is
the only member of this strange triad that I would want to
be friends with. What I'd like to chat to Frankl about, if I
could invite him to a dinner party, is the nature of meaning.
What makes a life meaningful? What does it *mean* for a
life to be meaningful? That second question is very meta, I
know, but we do have to ask it. I want to get some kind of a
handle on what I'm talking about when I talk about living a
meaningful life.

"In the Nazi concentration camps," Frankl writes, "one
could have witnessed that those who knew that there was a

task waiting for them to fulfill were most apt to survive." He saw that people who had a project that gave them a *reason* to live were more likely to do so, because they could see how there was a meaning in their continued life. But Frankl emphasizes that not any old project would be relevant. A task or project of the kind that could make life worth living had to be focused on something other than oneself.

It might be other people, it might be a work of art, it might be a career. What exactly it was didn't matter so much; there just had to be something that pointed beyond the narrow horizons of the individual. Frankl says that "a man who becomes conscious of the responsibility he bears towards a human being who affectionately waits for him, or to an unfinished work, will never be able to throw away his life."

Frankl's ideas in this respect have a deep intuitive appeal to me. I don't care about having nice feelings the way I care about my life being eudaimonic. Don't get me wrong – it's not that I don't want nice feelings. (I've spent enough time living with depression to know what they're worth and what it's like to miss them.) It's just that, to me, it doesn't seem as if nice feelings are the point of living. I can survive without them. If I am in a state of eudaimonia, I still have reasons to live. And, in addition to their resonance with *my* experience, because of what *Frankl* experienced I get the sense that words such as his are spoken with some authority.

The responses to the Paradox of Happiness offered by Frankl and J. S. Mill have something crucial in common. Both thinkers suggest that the resolution must point outwards, beyond the individual, to other people or to larger projects. (This is another important cautionary note against trying to press eudaimonia into service as a simplistic "quick fix" for the paradox: aiming at one's own eudaimonia is individualistic and inward-looking, just as aiming at one's own happiness is.) The seventeenth-century metaphysical poet John Donne gestures in the same direction when he famously says (in his *Devotions upon Emergent Occasions*): "No man is an island, entire of itself; every man is a piece of the continent, a part of the main. . . . Any man's death diminishes me, because I am involved in mankind."

More prosaically, enforced total isolation (i.e. solitary confinement) is a form of torture.[9] Even less extreme, more commonplace kinds of loneliness can be severely detrimental to human health. A good survey of recent research on the deadly effects of isolation is provided by the American Psychological Association.[10] As summarized by the APA, one meta-analysis finds the "lack of social connection heightens health risks as much as smoking 15 cigarettes a day or having alcohol use disorder," while a 2019 study finds that "social isolation increases the risk of premature death from every cause for every race."

Putting this together with some of Frankl's ideas outlined above suggests that what is so devastating about isolation is that it interferes with meaning-making. With no collaborations, interactions or projects that point beyond oneself, one is unable to find or create any meaning in one's life, and Frankl argued from observation that meaning can make the difference between life and death. The empirical evidence in support of this latter point is also starting to build; for example, one 2019 study found that having a "stronger purpose in life" was correlated with "decreased mortality."[11]

If meaning is – at least for most of us, most of the time – *collaborative*, that would explain why isolation is deadly. We can, however, reasonably ask whether the others with whom one collaborates in making meaning have to be *human* others. I don't see why other beings shouldn't also be able to play the role – non-human animals might be enough company for some of us. Perhaps deities, or the ubiquitous consciousnesses posited by the panpsychist, could also play the required role if they exist. And maybe (although this is more of a stretch) having the right kind of emotional or spiritual relationship to something abstract – art or music itself, for example – could be enough, if it enabled the requisite sense of collaboration and creativity. At any rate, I don't want to rule out these possibilities. But it's safe to say that most people cannot thrive without at least some human contact.

Under the influence of a few centuries of individualistic capitalism and several decades of American cultural hegemony, our conception of happiness has become a hedonic, individualistic one. We are also constantly told that happiness is at the core of a good life and that happiness should be our primary life goal. The Paradox of Happiness results: we pursue our own individualistic happiness, and this does not make us happy.

Instead, let's see what happens if we say that a good life is a eudaimonic life. Eudaimonia, in the old sense, is about being surrounded by good spirits. Good people, healthy environments, positive influences, supportive communities and networks. As I see it, a proper understanding of eudaimonia demands, as a baseline, that we take into account the deep and dramatic implications of our interconnectedness: we find *meaning* in collaboration and creation, and meaning is what makes life worth living for us.

Happiness might be a side effect of eudaimonia. As J. S. Mill puts it: "[a]iming . . . at something else, [we] find happiness by the way." Or, in Frankl's terms: "happiness cannot be pursued; it must ensue." Eudaimonia does not *guarantee* happiness, but that's OK, because happiness is not the be-all and end-all. It doesn't define what a good life consists in.

Crucially, a proper understanding of eudaimonia helps us see why neither happiness nor eudaimonia itself should be positioned as a generic life goal or something to be "pursued" for its own sake. Sharpening our understanding of eudaimonia gives us a conceptual tool that we can use to *think* about what goals to pursue in our lives, but one's own eudaimonia cannot *be* the goal. Eudaimonia-inducing, meaning-making goals must instead be outward-looking: interactive, creative and collaborative. The details of what those goals look like will be different for all of us, but that's OK too. We are better off without those old-style, one-size-fits-all philosophies of "human nature."

Given that we all have different goals, we all need to be able to make our own choices in order to advance our goals. Viktor Frankl argues – and I agree with him – that finding meaning in life is strongly tied to self-determination and having the freedom to choose.

Frankl also says that this kind of freedom can never be completely lost, even in the direst of situations: "Everything can be taken from a man but one thing, the last of the human freedoms – to choose one's attitude in any given set of circumstances, to choose one's own way."[12] He presents this point as an argument against losing hope. But this is where I have questions. For one thing, the freedom to choose one's own attitude is a complicated thing, given how suggestible and responsive to the opinions of others humans can be. My main worry, though, is that it's a very *limited* kind of freedom. Is it enough to make your life meaningful, if you have no other freedoms beyond that?

Frankl says – and again, I agree with him on this – that the kind of goal that makes a life meaningful has to be something that points beyond the individual. But for that very reason, it seems to me, you can't pursue such a task completely on your own or in a totally antagonistic environment. It has to involve others or be able to have some kind of larger impact on the world. If you were utterly prevented from interacting with other people, or with whatever parts of your environment your project requires you to collaborate with and/or influence, then you would not be able to pursue your meaning-giving tasks. You could choose your attitude towards that awful situation, but I don't see how that could be enough, because I don't see how that would salvage the meaning of the work itself. Being in an *entirely* hostile situation results in a total collapse of meaningful possibilities for one's future.

Working on the projects that can give life meaning is, in that sense, always a kind of collaboration. Whether it's a collaboration with other people or with more abstract forces, even with the universe itself, it's never just a matter of one individual doing their thing. Likewise, I want to say, whether a life is worth living is not – cannot be – determined entirely by the individual living it. To live a life worth living, we need an atmosphere that's at least vaguely conducive to our being able to pursue our meaningful projects. In the metaphor that frames this chapter, we need to be surrounded by good-enough daimons.

## Eudaimonia vs. the Romantic Paradox

If a proper understanding of eudaimonia is the sparkly crystal center of the Paradox of Happiness, what's hiding inside the Romantic Paradox?

The Romantic Paradox, to recap, says that chasing the romantic "happy ever after" tends to make us unhappy. Or, in the style of J. S. Mill: "those only are happy ever after who have their minds fixed on some object other than their own happiness ever after."

The romantic, feelings-first conception of love encourages us to think of love as an intense emotional state, either excruciating agony (sad love) or blissful pleasure (happy ever after love). This is what, on my diagnosis, gives rise to the Romantic Paradox: we end up pursuing something (those blissfully happy feelings) that philosophers have been trying to tell us for centuries cannot be pursued. In the Romantic case there are exacerbating factors too, as I mentioned in chapter 2, with the most important being the static nature of romantic love (the "ever after" part of happy ever after).

I think the crystalline heart of the Romantic Paradox is similar to that of the Paradox of Happiness: a proper understanding of eudaimonia. But, in the Romantic case, we will need, more specifically, a proper understanding of eudaimonic love. Throughout the rest of this book, I'll be working on developing that. But it may be helpful to sketch its outlines here.

Like eudaimonia in general, eudaimonic love is about the collaborative creation of meaning. It is not individualistic but outward-looking, and by this I don't mean simply each loving partner looking outward towards the other(s), but also that eudaimonic love looks outward beyond the relationship and works in collaboration with its context, community and environment in meaningful ways. Eudaimonic love is good-spirited love, or love with *good daimons*, and the relevant daimons include not just those of the individuals and that of the loving relationship itself but the larger daimons at work around the relationship, creating the conditions that are necessary for love.

Eudaimonic love is emphatically *dynamic*, not static like romantic love. The daimon of a loving relationship must be understood as something that grows and changes, like a living creature. Something that is impacted by its environment. Eudaimonic love is also not defined by any particular kinds of feelings or emotions, and this means it has room for the full gamut of human emotional potential. If we achieve eudaimonic love, happiness ever after might ensue, or it might not. If it doesn't, it's OK, because happiness is no longer the *point*. Sad love is not necessarily a failure condition. Sadness – and other "negative" emotions – can be a legitimate part of one's love story.

Intriguingly, Plato called Eros himself a "daimon." In ancient Greek culture, Eros was often thought of as a god – specifically, the god of love, passion, sexuality and desire. In the oldest traditions Eros was among the primeval forces involved in the creation of the universe, but later he is made the son of Aphrodite: a youthful deity, as opposed to an ancient one. But in Plato's famous dialogue *Symposium*, Eros is called a daimon in order to mark him out as a semi-divine spirit, halfway between a god and a mortal.

While I imagine it couldn't hurt if the daimon Eros smiled on one's relationships, the conception of eudaimonic love I have in mind is quite a bit more complicated. It's not so much a matter of being favoured by a god (or semi-divine entity) of love, more a project that requires the co-operation of *various* good spirits, most of which look quite mundane by comparison. The attitude of your friends, for example, or the prevailing political attitude towards relationships of the kind you're in. These are the kinds of daimons that I'm saying must be good (or at least good enough) if love is to thrive.

Like eudaimonia in general, eudaimonic love is connected in some important ways to agency and freedom to choose. As Frankl argued, finding life meaningful requires having the freedom to choose and pursue one's meaningful goals and projects. Unlike Frankl, I think this freedom can be lost – in that sense, one's spirit can be killed by completely unco-operative environments. I think the same is true for love, too: the spirit of a loving relationship can be killed by a sufficiently toxic atmosphere, even if the people in the relationship are doing everything right. Imagine trying to make a loving relationship work between two men in Victorian England or an interracial relationship in 1950s America. Love in these contexts did not have the freedom it needed to thrive – or, in many such cases, even survive.

As I develop my ideas around eudaimonic love and its application to the Romantic Paradox, it will be helpful to position it alongside a few of its most significant influences. First among these is the work of bell hooks on the nature of love.

The Romantic conception of love has not gone unchallenged throughout its history. bell hooks is one of the most powerful recent advocates for an opposing view. As hooks understands it, feeling is not "first" in the way e e cummings suggests. Rather, she argues, love is a matter not of how you feel but of what you *do*.[13] It is active rather than passive:

something we choose rather than something that happens to us. Our autonomy and our agency are paramount. Love, on this unromantic conception, doesn't hit you like a bolt out of the blue, and you don't "fall" in love like you fall into a hole in the ground. It has nothing to do with sitting around dreaming of the "some day" when your "prince will come."

In fact, the active conception of love has existed at least since the middle of the twentieth century, but always on the margins. It has lost out to the romantic conception in that it has not become culturally dominant, but it does have its defenders. hooks is working within a tradition that includes psychologist Eric Fromm,[14] psychiatrist M. Scott Peck[15] and Martin Luther King, who once urged that "love is not this sentimental something that we talk about . . . not merely an emotional something."[16] Some philosophers have also theorized love in terms of "concern" for another or a desire for their well-being,[17] although hooks – to my mind more convincingly – lists concern as just one of what she calls the "ingredients" of active love, along with respect, care, trust, recognition, honest communication, and others.

## Job-crafting

A second major influence comes from a less predictable quarter: the world of work. Let me explain why. When I started thinking about the philosophy of love, I found that many people were embarrassed to talk about love in public[18] – as if it were too personal, or too private, or even too *silly* a topic for polite company. (Unfortunately, the people I least wanted to hear from were typically the ones who didn't seem to feel this way.) When I read contemporary philosophers on love, I also find them theorizing it in an oddly detached manner, as if it could be considered as pure theory, and as if they did not bring to the discussion a life's worth of emotional baggage. There are some cultural spaces held open for love's messier and fleshier aspects – romance novels, romcoms, emotionally overwrought pop music, and so on. But many of these are feminized – romcoms are positioned as "chick flicks," for example – and none of them are generally taken seriously. They tend to be "guilty pleasures" at best.

It seems much more acceptable to talk publicly about one's *career* than about one's love life. I suspect that's because work is already conceived as public, reasonable and masculine. Whatever the reason, I think this disparity is a pretty sad reflection on who and what we are as a society. But it does mean that the shared concepts we have for understanding our work lives are in certain respects more developed than those we have for understanding our love lives. And this can be useful. So, strange as it may sound, at this point I'm going to step over to the world of work in search of lessons about love and to make good on the idea that a proper understanding of eudaimonic love can free us from the Romantic Paradox and its associated bad dreams.

The relevance of work has to do with that idea that exercising one's autonomy in the pursuit of one's goals is an essential requirement for living a meaningful life. Most workers have roles that are prescribed and circumscribed by job descriptions and employment contracts. That is to say, they don't have complete freedom and autonomy in deciding what work to do. They have to do what they're paid to do. What happens to our autonomy – and finding meaning – under those kinds of constraints? If we learn more about that, it might help us better understand what happens to autonomy and meaning under the kinds of constraints that typically surround romantic relationships. This isn't as much of a stretch as it might sound: in many ways, when we take on a role such as "boyfriend" or "wife," it comes with a tacitly understood "job description" attached.

The theoretical insight that interests me concerns *jobcrafting*. The concept of job-crafting was introduced by Amy Wrzesniewski and Jane Dutton in 2001 to describe "actions employees take to shape, mold, and re-define their jobs."[19] This is how Wrzesniewski describes one of the workers who provided the original motivation for the theory:[20]

> one of the members of the [university hospital] clean-ing crew we talked with worked on a floor that cared for patients who were in comas . . . and in describing the tasks that were part of her job, she described taking down the pictures that hung in the hospital patients' rooms on a regular basis and moving them around, switching them around between rooms. And when we asked her why it was she did this, she said that her thought was perhaps some-thing about changing some aspect in the environment of the patients, though they were unconscious, might spark recovery in some way. We became very intrigued by this and asked, "Is this part of your role, given that you work on this kind of floor?" And what she told us was: "That's not part of my job, but that's part of me."

Research on job-crafting is often positioned as a contribution to "positive organizational psychology," a business-oriented subfield of positive psychology (which I discussed in chapter 1). But I am inclined to think job-crafting is about more than just psychology, never mind positive organizational psychology. There is a philosophical lesson here.

The hospital cleaner moving pictures around the patients' rooms is offered as an example of one specific form of job-crafting, which the researchers call *task*-crafting – adjusting the actual tasks performed in the course of one's work. They also mention two other forms that job-crafting can take. First there's *relational* crafting, which is about forging work relationships that change (or go beyond) formal job descriptions. And then there's *cognitive* crafting, which is about . . . well, it's kind of about the meaning of life.

No, really. Cognitive crafting, as Wrzesniewski puts it, is about "how people perceive the tasks and their meaning."

Job-crafting "gives people an opportunity to have their own agentic impact on . . . their contribution to the organization, to the world, the role of work in their life."[21] What exactly is an "agentic impact" and why is it such a big deal? Well, in simple language, it means taking action – doing something on purpose, something we've chosen to do – and having that action make a difference. As for why that's such a big deal, let me first pull some neuroscience into the picture.

Dopamine is often thought of as the brain's reward system. It can make us feel good. And one way to get a dopamine hit is by making choices, taking action and achieving goals. In *The Upward Spiral*,[22] Alex Korb explains that, in an fMRI study, "[a]ctively choosing . . . increased rewarding dopamine activity." He also says: "not only is dopamine released when you finally achieve a long-term goal but it's also released with each step you make as you move closer towards achieving it." If taking action feels good, the reverse is also true: feeling helpless, hopeless and unable to act, or even to make decisions, does *not* feel good. In fact, these are typical symptoms of depression.[23]

Building on this train of thought, we can assume that having an "agentic impact" at work probably *feels* good. It probably gets you a dopamine hit. And, indeed, research suggests that job-crafting can "bring about numerous positive outcomes, including engagement, job satisfaction, resilience and thriving."[24] So this is perhaps part of the explanation for why a hospital cleaner was moving pictures around between rooms – adding this task to her assigned role made her feel good, because she was more in control.

But that's not all. Job-crafting researchers explain how the process of crafting a job "creates opportunities for employees to experience the meaning of their work differently by aligning the job with their values, motivations, and beliefs."[25] And it's here, in this connection with *meaning*, that I think the deep philosophical lesson of job-crafting emerges. Something is going on here that may branch out into good feelings and dopamine rewards but also runs deeper than those things.

We can turn to Viktor Frankl again for help following up this lead. Frankl says that meaning is ultimately what makes a life worth living. Since most of us spend a substantial percentage of our waking hours working, being able to find one's work meaningful could make a huge difference to one's life.

Frankl also says that to find meaning in life one has to be oriented towards something beyond oneself. I mentioned earlier that, because of this, meaning-making is always in a sense collaborative. It depends on the people, the atmosphere, the Zeitgeists, the daimons around you. Being able to live a meaningful life is partly about whether the world is ready to let you make certain kinds of decisions, ready to respect them, ready to work with you to achieve something together. And the same is true for our working lives. Certain kinds of "job-crafting" won't make your work more satisfying and meaningful, they'll just get you fired. What you can get away with in terms of crafting your job really depends on your circumstances: Who's your boss? How strict is the company policy? Do you work in an office with a door you can close, or is it an "open-plan" cubicle?

But, to me, one of the most compelling facts about job-crafting is that people do it even when it *might* get them fired. Here is Wrzesniewski again:[26]

> In asking the cleaners about the kinds of things they were doing on the job . . . they talked about doing things like walking the elderly visitors of patients all the way back through the Byzantine structure of the hospital to their cars – which was an offence for which they could be fired – so that the visitors would not get lost, thus worrying the patient about whether their family members were OK.

## Love-crafting

The metaphor of "crafting" one's job sounds creative, and inspiring and useful. Perhaps even beautiful. None of these are things one might typically associate with paid employment, but the metaphor juxtaposes the world of work with the world of crafting and opens those associations up for us to explore. I find the metaphor suggestive and generative in all kinds of ways. For example, it lets us think of crafting a job being a bit like crafting a sculpture from a lump of clay. Maybe you don't have much say as to what lump of clay you get as your raw material, but you do get to decide how you're going to shape that thing once it's yours.

In an influential 1980 book called *Metaphors We Live By*,[27] linguists George Lakoff and Mark Johnson discuss how powerfully metaphors can shape our lives, often without our really noticing. And one of the examples they talk about is love. They explain that we often tend to use turbulent metaphors for love – metaphors such as *love is war* and *love is madness*. This is not surprising, given what I've said about the dominant romantic conception of love (where it's all about huge, overwhelming and uncontrollable feelings). But Lakoff and Johnson also argue that these are really not helpful metaphors, and that we'd be better off replacing them with this alternative: *love is a collaborative work of art*.

I really like this suggestion. I think this gives us yet another piece of the puzzle when it comes to understanding what eudaimonic love is, and especially how it's different from romantic love. If romantic love is war and madness, eudaimonic love is a collaborative work of art. I'm not even sure this is a metaphor: I think eudaimonic love might *literally* be a collaborative work of art, at least in some cases.

Thinking of eudaimonic love as a collaborative and creative practice sits perfectly alongside the ideas I canvassed above, namely that eudaimonic love is active, intentional and dynamic (whereas romantic love is passive, involuntary and static). Eudaimonic love is something we intentionally do, not something we *fall* into. Eudaimonic love isn't an unchanging happy ever after but an evolving, growing thing that can encompass the full range of human emotional experience.

When it comes to the details of what a collaborative practice of love amounts to, we can borrow the concept of *job-crafting* and give it a twist. People job-craft when they shape their work role – as determined by their job description – to better fit their values, their skills, and their sense of what is meaningful to them. People *love*-craft when they do the same with the "job" of lover or partner (or spouse or boyfriend or girlfriend or non-binary friend).

We can think of it this way: society hands out a standard, one-size-fits-all "job description" for the role of *romantic partner*. We all receive the same scripts, the same performance measures, the same ideal standards and best practices. They are informal, but we understand them very clearly and we know there are costs that come with breaking expectations. But sometimes our preferences, our goals, or even our identities, are *misaligned* with those expectations. This presents an opportunity for love-crafting.

To use myself as an example: I was handed a job description for *romantic partner* that included a very strong requirement that a partner should be monogamous. I thought – because I was taught to think – that any other kind of relationship would be immoral and disgusting. In practicing polyamorous love, I am love-crafting in the sense that I'm reshaping the role of *partner* to better fit my values, my skills, and my sense of what is meaningful to me. Love-crafting is a way I can make my loving relationships – and ultimately my life – more meaningful.

The metaphor of love-crafting also enables me push back against the idea that being polyamorous makes me a "rebel." I don't want to be a rebel, and I don't care for the belligerent metaphor *norm-breaking is rebellion*. I far prefer the creative metaphor *norm-breaking is love-crafting*.

I also dislike the metaphor *norm-breaking is experimenting*. People often call polyamory an "experiment in living" or describe non-monogamous relationships as "experimental." But this is to present them as unstable, risky, liable to fail. When people call my relationships "experimental" it sounds as if I'm just trying something out, going through a phase that I'll get over when I revert to being "normal" (safe and non-experimental).

My relationships are not experiments, except perhaps in the sense that everything we do in life is an experiment. And I'm not a rebel – at least, I'm not trying to be one. Describing non-monogamous love as "experimental" and "rebellious" sounds to me as if it's designed to put people off the idea of doing it. To classify me as a *rebel* is to call attention to how different I am from "normal" people. And calling my relationships "experimental" makes them sound as if they're unsafe. Using the wrong metaphors makes something that I experience as creative and life-affirming appear dangerous and difficult.

The metaphors operate as a kind of illusion or a piece of conceptual misdirection. Where *love-crafting* sets us free, *rebel* keeps us in line. Where *love-crafting* empowers us to challenge established norms and to be creative, *experimental* shuts us down by raising the spectre of a "failed" experiment.

When it hands me an implicit job description for *partner*, society thinks it is the boss of me. And, in a sense, it's right. Society *is* the boss of me, as long as I want to belong to it and participate in it. If I want to keep my position (as it were) I have to grant a certain amount of authority to the social order that governs my corner of time and space. But that doesn't mean I have no autonomy to structure my life within those parameters, or even to push back against the parameters themselves. As I mentioned above, the researchers studying job-crafting found it was happening even in situations where it was explicitly forbidden and could lead to someone getting fired. Love-crafting is the same. Some people will break the "rules" for what a relationship should be, because it's important. It *means* something. People love-craft even when they risk being "fired" – when it amounts to breaking the law, for example. The criminalization of male homosexuality in the UK didn't stop men falling in love with each other, although the consequences of being found out could be devastating.

Some employers are more open to job-crafting than others. One way employers can positively *encourage* job-crafting is through the strategic use of periodic reviews. These can be used not simply as assessments of how well the employee is performing according to predetermined standards but as opportunities to discuss how the job might be made a better fit for the employee's strengths and motivations.[28]

In the world of love, an analogue for this kind of review process has arisen organically: the renewable relationship contract. Mandy Len Catron maintains an annually renewable relationship contract with her partner Mark, covering everything from the division of household tasks to their big future plans. When it's time to renew their contract, Catron and her partner set aside time to consider how they, and their relationship, are changing over time. I see this as them *crafting* their relationship, to get the best fit with their values and passions and strengths as they are. (Not as they were when they first met, or as they are expected to be.) They communicate and collaborate in pursuit of their shared creative project: they are *making* their relationship – and their lives – together. A collaborative work of art.

Catron says in the *New York Times*: "Writing a relationship contract may sound calculating or unromantic, but every relationship is contractual; we're just making the terms more explicit. It reminds us that love isn't something that happens to us – it's something we're making together."[29] It's interesting that people find relationship contracts "unromantic." (Side bar: I seriously considered calling this book *Unromantic Love*.) Catron – like bell hooks, and Lakoff and Johnson, and me – is pushing back against the romantic conception of love as an uncontrollable passion and making room to understand love as something to be practiced thoughtfully and with intention.

Am I saying annually renewable relationship contracts will ensure that all our relationships become happy ever afters? Of course not. If you feel tempted to ask that question, you're still in the grip of the fairy tale, just trying to rewrite a part of it. The point is that there *is* no single approach to love that will (or could, or should) work for everyone. For that matter, not everyone is looking for a "happy ever after." Indeed, not everyone is looking for an *anything* ever after. Although we're all conditioned to expect a single romantic relationship to be our main source of personal happiness for ever, relationship therapist Esther Perel has laid out some serious problems with that expectation, which – as life expectancy increases – are only intensifying.[30] In tandem with the expectation that partners will be "everything" to each other, "failure" (often in the form of cheating) is very common, and its repercussions for partners and children can be devastating.

There is nothing broken about wanting something different. This is diversity. It's the uniformity of our romantic narrative that is broken: the fact that we are all supplied with the same pre-written, one-size-fits-all "love story" script. That leaves us poorly prepared to deal with the panoply of *true* love stories, the rich and abundant fountain of all our real lives and real loves. The diversity of human love will not be forced into a narrow channel. It is overflowing everywhere.

I love-craft by designing a non-monogamous relationship structure with my partners. Some people do it by developing a network of loving friendships and family relationships without a focal partner. Others do it by entering into "normal" or "traditional" relationships. This last part is really important: you don't *have* to change the script to practice love intentionally. It makes all the difference in the world to renew the terms of your contract unchanged *because you read them and you decided you didn't want to change anything*, rather than because you couldn't be bothered to look at them and anyway you heard that change was impossible.

Our best hope of achieving eudaimonic love is to craft our loving relationships with intention, and in collaboration with our partners, to bring those relationships into alignment with what we truly value, what we truly desire from one another, and what we are truly in a position to offer to one another.

This isn't always possible. It may be prevented by negative forces – bad daimons – of various kinds: the law, our culture, peer pressure and internalized conditioning, to name just a few. But in the right circumstances – with nurturing, supportive daimons of community and culture surrounding us – we may be able to fine-tune our relationships so that they resonate with the *core* of our own and our partners' true selves. In return, well-tuned relationships can nurture and support those wider daimons of time and place: a community comprised of miserable people forced into "traditional" marriages that don't work for them is (all too familiarly) a toxic environment for all involved. Whereas one that is full of diverse, genuine, loving relationships encourages more of the same. Most real-life environments fall somewhere in between. But a wide range of variation is possible within the two extremes, and it is always worth fighting to nudge the dial a little in the right direction.

There's just one problem with being fortunate – "hap"py – enough to experience the freedom to choose how to love. This freedom comes with the *responsibility* to choose wisely. Once we question the assumption that everyone is looking for a romantic "happy ever after" with its traditional script, how do we decide what goals are *really* important to us, in life and in love?

How can we know our own minds and, no less importantly, our own hearts?

# 4

# Know Thyself

## Choice problems

In ideal circumstances, we would be free to love-craft our own relationships: to choose who and how to love without constraints. Not only external constraints, such as peer pressure and social stigma, but also internal constraints: our own baggage and hang-ups. The little daimons in our heads that tell us we aren't "good enough" for that person, or that loving the way we do is shameful, or whatever else they can think of to shut us down and make us feel inadequate.

Like external daimons, our own internal daimons can be powerful influences, whether good or bad, nourishing or toxic. And those toxic internal daimons can be every bit as much a barrier to freely choosing our own way in love as toxic external daimons such as cultural stereotyping or parents who won't accept your orientation. In fact, they tend get on well together – toxic environments will easily spawn negative self-talk, and in return those little daimons in our heads make us less likely to stand up for ourselves and challenge the external toxicity.

Our internal daimons may be inside our own minds, but that doesn't mean we control them. At least, not in any straightforward sense. One doesn't just *decide* to stop feeling romantically inadequate or to reject the prejudices one was raised with. It is work. And the first part of the work is knowing what work there is to do. In other words, we need to know ourselves. Knowing ourselves is a crucial part of talking back to those internal daimons that can stand in the way of exercising our own autonomy in love, having the freedom to make the choices in love that really matter. The ones that can make love – and life – meaningful.

The maxim "know thyself" was carved on the temple of Apollo in Delphi. People came to the temple at Delphi to visit the Pythian oracle, a priestess who delivered prophecies in the form of (what appeared to be) rambling nonsense but was interpreted as divine, mystical guidance. Her temple was not only a sacred place but one of deep epistemological reflection. An audience with the oracle would be sought by powerful leaders of the era when they were in the throes of making their biggest, most important decisions. An instruction carved into the temple of the Pythia meant something. It wasn't a casual suggestion. But it's not the easiest instruction to follow.

In addition to the issues created by the daimons in our heads, I want to call attention to two more problems with freely choosing love, both of which also point to a need to know ourselves. These two aren't about restrictions on the choices available to you – rather, they are intrinsic to the act of choosing.

In fact, the second problem is the *opposite* of restriction: choice overload. Maybe you've heard of the "jam study"? This study was published in 2000,[1] and it's been highly influential ever since. Basically, the researchers found that people were about ten times more likely to buy some jam when there were six kinds of jam to choose from than when there were twenty-four kinds.[2] Faced with too much choice, they simply didn't choose at all. Having lots of choices open to you may lead only to confusion or to the dreaded FOMO. Or choosing might just start to seem like too much effort.

If you've ever found yourself swiping through endless profiles on a dating website, you might be familiar with that feeling of choice overload as applied to the romantic context. Love researcher Helen Fisher, interviewed for *Time* magazine in 2018, warns of this possibility: "You meet so many people that you can't decide and make no decision at all," Fisher says. To keep yourself in check, Fisher suggests limiting your pool of potential dates to somewhere between five and nine people, rather than swiping endlessly. "After that, the brain starts to go into cognitive overload, and you don't choose anybody."[3]

The problem with this kind of advice is that there's no one-size-fits-all approach to dealing either with choice fatigue or with dating. Some people may be best served by focusing on just one person at a time. Others might do better with a time-based restriction than a numerical one. But, to know where you fall, you need to *know yourself.*

Research suggests a few specific ways individuals might differ when it comes to romantic choice overload. In a more comprehensive follow-up to the original jam study,[4] researchers found that, while more choice impedes choice-making under certain conditions, the effect wasn't uniform across all circumstances. For example, people who placed a high value on making a quick, easy selection were more likely to be put off by having lots of choices. But when there was an easy way to identify a top contender, the presence of lots of other, less-good, choices available didn't have as much of an impact. Crucially, having lots of choices presented more of a problem when people were *less sure of what they wanted.* Knowing yourself – in particular, knowing what you want – is an important part of dealing with choice overload issues.[5]

A third problem – which can interact with choice overload but can also manifest separately – is having high standards. Not just any high standards, but a particular kind of high standard: wanting *the best available.* "Maximizers" are people who tend to fret about making the best possible choice in a given situation, whereas "satisficers" live by the rule that *good enough is good enough.* It's typically easier to tell when something's good enough than whether it's the best available, so maximizers typically have a harder time choosing than do satisficers. It's easy to see how a drive to "maximize" one's romantic prospects can quickly degenerate

into those cycles of endless swiping. There's always someone else to meet – what if they're *better*?[6] (This issue most
squarely impacts monogamous dating, but since that is the
normative kind, it is a common problem.)

If we tie this last point back to the idea that making
choices and taking action leads to dopamine rewards, which
make us feel good, and if we bear in mind that "happiness" in the contemporary sense is all about good feelings
and positive emotions, we might expect satisficers to be,
on the average, living "happier" lives. And, indeed, a 2002
study found that "maximizers reported significantly less life
satisfaction, happiness, optimism, and self-esteem, and significantly more regret and depression, than did satisficers."[7]

This doesn't mean the satisficers are choosing better, or
more wisely – not once we are willing to question the received
wisdom that happiness is the defining feature of love and a
good life. But it does suggest that we might be able to assess
our own choices more clearly by knowing whether we are
maximizers or satisficers (remembering, of course, that we
might change over time or between contexts). If you're more
of a satisficer, it's good to remember that a choice might
make you happy without necessarily being a good, wise or
meaningful one. Conversely, if you're more of a maximizer,
it might be pertinent to bear in mind that choices which
*don't* make you happy aren't necessarily bad. This is important in connection with the idea that eudaimonic love has
space for the full range of human emotions – including
sadness. (We will come back to this in chapter 5.)

A study published in 2013 found that "[h]appiness was
linked to being a taker rather than a giver, whereas meaningfulness went with being a giver rather than a taker."[8] As
defined by these researchers, "happiness" once again means
"an experiential state that contains a globally positive affec-
tive tone" – or, in simpler words, an overall nice feeling.
Right now, in 2021, we are perhaps especially well placed
to understand the gross moral dangers of treating life's

biggest takers as its biggest winners or viewing such people as models to emulate. (Must one imagine Donald Trump happy?) I'm not suggesting that giving is necessarily better than taking, or that we should aim at one to the exclusion of the other. But there may be something to be said for striking a balance, or at least not assuming that being a happy taker is the same as living a good life.

In all these ways and more, knowing ourselves is a precondition for eudaimonic love: that is, for practicing love in a way that respects and responds to who we truly are, and what makes our lives truly meaningful. Are you a maximizer or a satisficer? A giver or a taker? How do you deal with choice fatigue? And perhaps the most important, but also the most challenging: what do your internal daimons sound like?

These are just a few of the kinds of self-knowledge that can be key in romantic contexts. There are many more. But I hope the few I've surveyed are enough to establish that "know thyself" is a multifaceted and complex demand.

## Search for the hero inside yourself

We shouldn't assume that we can figure out everything there is to know about ourselves just by introspection: that is, by "looking inside." However easy it might *seem* to know ourselves from the inside, that easiness is all too often an illusion.

Humans – normal, healthy, humans – suffer from all sorts of cognitive biases, distortions, self-deceptions and irrationalities that can seriously interfere with our self-knowledge. For example, confirmation biases lead us to seek out evidence that supports what we already believe but ignore evidence to the contrary. If we're already convinced we're worthless, for example, we tend to overlook the evidence that we're not. Or consider the "moral licensing" effect, a psychological twist that makes us liable to act *badly* in situations where we *feel* ourselves to be especially virtuous. There are many, many more examples of this kind of thing.[9]

And when it comes to knowing ourselves, our cognitive biases seem to go into overdrive. One of the most interesting groups of cognitive biases in this connection are the *self-serving* biases. Self-serving biases are like looking at ourselves through rose-tinted glasses. They make us consistently over-estimate our skills, achievements, virtues and life situation in general but consistently underestimate our failings and shortcomings, as well as the chances of bad things happening to us. It's now a well-confirmed empirical finding that, for any positive attribute, people typically rate themselves "above average" in that attribute.[10] Of course, that's not how averages work. When we "search for the hero inside ourselves," we tend to find one, even if there isn't really one there.

Lacking self-awareness can be a problem in life generally, and in love specifically. Our level of self-awareness can make or break our romantic relationships. Many of us have had experiences with romantic partners who do not communicate their needs, not because they are being dishonest but because they simply don't know what those needs are. And, of course, many of us have had experiences of being that partner.

Attaining self-knowledge, however, is not only work but often challenging and unpleasant work. Seeing ourselves as we really are doesn't always feel good. In that sense, it is set at odds with American positivity culture and the pursuit of happiness.

The psychological thesis known as "depressive realism"[11] holds that a group of people we think of as "unwell" – namely the clinically depressed – are (on average) more accurate in their perceptions of themselves and their situations than are supposedly "healthy" or "normal" individuals. In a nuanced discussion of depressive realism in the context of contemporary positivity culture, philosopher and psychoanalyst Julie Reshe writes:[12]

Look around and you'll notice we demand a state of per-manent happiness from ourselves and others. The ten-dency that goes together with overpromotion of happiness is stigmatisation of the opposite of happiness – emotional suffering, such as depression, anxiety, grief or disappoint-ment. We label emotional suffering a deviation and a problem, a distortion to be eliminated – a pathology in need of treatment. The voice of sadness is censored as sick.

She compares depression to "a fever that can be scary in the moment but isn't inherently bad" because it promotes a crucial healing process. Like a fever, depression may impair everyday performance and feel bad, but these are traded off against its benefits in terms of accurate analysis of one's real situation and real problems. While they may prop up our egos and keep us happy, self-serving biases are a serious problem when it comes to knowing ourselves. Reshe contin-ues: "superficial states of happiness are largely a way not to be alive. Mental health, positive psychology and dominant therapy modalities such as CBT all require that we remain silent and succumb to our illusions until we die."

Unlike romantic love, which is founded on a beautiful happy fantasy, *eudaimonic* love must be consistent with reality, including all its "negative" aspects. Eudaimonic love will often be sad, simply because sadness is often the appro-priate emotional response to reality.[13] My view – resonant with what Reshe is saying here – is that much of the value of sad love lies precisely in its accuracy and its responsive-ness to the truth. Only when we take off the rose-tinted spectacles – something many "healthy" people will not and perhaps cannot do – can we see people as they really are. And only then can we *love* them as they really are: I cannot love someone if I see only an idealized, distorted version of them, because in that case I do not *know* the person I purport to love.

This applies to self-love as much as to love of another person. Self-knowledge is necessary in a relationship, then, not just for communicating one's needs, but because without it self-*love* is impossible. And when we do not love ourselves we are rarely able to love another person – or, indeed, live – in a meaningful way.

Unfortunately, though, self-serving biases represent just one tiny corner of our unconscious mental and emotional life, the full extent of which is so vast that it looks liable to render true self-knowledge not merely challenging but almost laughably impossible. Starting in the 1890s, Sigmund Freud[14] developed the idea that there are powerful, ever-present factors influencing our feelings and our decisions but that these are entirely opaque to us. This idea of a subconscious mind has evolved into an ever-expanding field of contemporary research that lays bare some deep holes in our self-awareness. Here's how psychologists Elizabeth Dunn and Michael Norton sum up the current state of play: "Fifty years of psychological research has shown that most of the 'action' in human thought and emotion takes place beneath the level of conscious awareness – and so trying to uncover the causes of your own happiness through introspection is like trying to perform your own heart transplant."[15] *Most of the action* in our mental and emotional lives is not accessible just by "searching inside" ourselves. That's quite a claim. How, then, am I supposed to know what I want, or what I need, or even *who I am* when it comes to love?

In saying that we shouldn't try to know ourselves primarily through direct introspection, Dunn and Norton are going up against a very influential tradition in Anglo-American philosophy according to which "looking inside ourselves" is actually our best and safest route to knowledge. According to some, it is even *infallible*.[16] This tradition is grounded in the work of René Descartes, a French philosopher from the early seventeenth century. His famous maxim *cogito ergo sum* (in English, "I think, therefore I am") was the upshot of his "method of doubt."[17] This involved rejecting everything about which he could entertain any doubt whatsoever, then rebuilding his entire belief system from its very foundations. Descartes felt as if he had reached that secure foundation when he noticed he could not doubt that he was thinking. From this, he reasoned, it must surely follow that he existed. "I think," he told himself, "therefore I am." His own direct experience – of his own thinking mind – struck him as the thing of which he could be most certain.

From Descartes onwards, philosophers working under his influence have tended to assume that self-knowledge is special: that it is easier to obtain, and more secure, than any other kind of knowledge about the rest of the world. But, as we have seen, the idea that we are good at knowing our own minds has been repeatedly called into serious question by an increasingly sophisticated empirical and conceptual understanding of the how the mind really works.

There's another intriguing kind of objection to Descartes, too, that dates back much earlier than Freud. In the intervening centuries, other philosophers[18] were already objecting that Descartes had no business using the word "I" in his famous phrase "I think, therefore I am" (or, in Latin, using the first-person verbs *cogito* and *sum*). Maybe Descartes could not coherently doubt that there was some kind of thinking going on, but how could he presume to know what kind of thing was *doing* the thinking? In other words, how could he know *himself*?

Dunn and Norton are relatively optimistic that there are ways to understand the subconscious parts of ourselves. But this knowledge, as they see it, comes through the expertise of others – the equivalent of having a trained surgeon to perform your heart transplant for you.

I'm not so confident that there are any experts ready to perform the procedures needed to know oneself. My reasons have to do with some deep methodological concerns I have about the science of ourselves. Let me explain.

## If it makes you happy (why the hell are you so sad)?

Why do we sing "If you're happy and you know it, clap your hands?" I guess if you're happy and you *don't* know it, you don't clap? But who could be happy and not know it?

Maybe we tend to overestimate ourselves and overlook many of the complexities of our subconscious minds. But – you might think – if you're happy, surely you can tell *that*. At a minimum, knowledge of our own basic emotions should be a relatively solid foundation for other kinds of self-knowledge.

Or is it? Here is a cautionary tale.

There is a so-called happiness gap between conservatives and liberals. Various statistical findings suggest that conservatives are happier than liberals. This looks to be a fairly robust situation, of long standing. In 2006, the Pew Research Center went so far as to publish a report claiming that, in the USA, "Republicans have been happier than Democrats every year since the General Social Survey began taking its measurements in 1972."[19] Why would that be the case? One off-the-cuff explanation is that conservatives don't want change, so that must mean they are happy with things the way they are. Liberals, by contrast, see the status quo as unsatisfactory and seek to change it. But it isn't necessarily like that. Conservatives may *resist* change that is actually happening or has recently happened. They may be *un*happy with the way things are now, instead seeking a return to a (real or imagined) golden era of the past. The slogan "Make America Great Again" advocates such a return. It is not an expression of happiness with the *current* status quo but with some (hypothetically "great") former time. A 2008 study advanced the subtler hypothesis that "conservatives (more than liberals) possess an ideological buffer against the negative hedonic effects of economic inequality."[20] In other words, if something in your belief system enables you to *justify* inequality, it doesn't make you feel so bad. And conservatives seem to be more able to justify inequality than liberals.

But this "happiness gap" research was all about *self-reported* happiness. Look at what happened when another study, published in 2015, took a different approach.[21] This time the researchers analyzed both self-reported happiness levels *and* other, more external, ways of measuring happiness. They looked at such things as how much the subjects used positive emotional vocabulary or appeared with genuine smiles in photographs. They found that, although the conservatives were happier if you went by what people said about themselves, when the external measures were used, it was the *liberals* who showed up as being happier. And, what's more, the original differences in self-reported happiness seemed to be fully accounted for by a "self-enhancing" style that is independently associated with conservatism. In other words, conservatives are more likely to talk themselves up in all sorts of ways.

So can we trust them when they also say they're happier? Aren't the external measures a bit more objective? Then again, seeing someone smiling in photos and writing upbeat posts on Twitter doesn't *prove* that the person is happy, any more than their ticking the "very happy" box on your questionnaire does. Sad people smile too. What we see of each other is inevitably partial. We see only what someone expresses or makes available to us. We must draw our own conclusions about what it means. And, unfortunately, humans aren't always great at doing this. We rely on stereotypes: we might assume, for example, that a depressed person is easily identifiable because they look sad. The stereotypical image of a person with depression is sometimes called the "head-clutcher." If you've read any (lazily illustrated) media articles about mental illness recently, you probably know what that looks like.[22]

So which is the true picture: what we say about ourselves, or what others see? The methodologically devastating truth is that it's probably neither. Our perceptions of happiness – whether our own *or* someone else's – are really shaky.

But wait, there's more. How's this for a methodologically unsettling finding. In one experiment conducted by Daniel Kahneman and Alan Kruger, participants were asked to photocopy a sheet of paper, and half of them found a dime on the copier machine. Those ten cents proved enough to make a substantial difference in how satisfied people said they were with their lives.[23] And another study, reported in the same article, found that people's self-reported happiness was often "strongly affected by earlier questions in a survey." So it starts to look as if anyone could quite easily manipulate the results of a happiness research study simply by inserting certain kinds of questions earlier in the survey. They could do this on purpose or they could do it by accident.

Either way, what it means is that a lot of the most important work has to be done in the process of *interpreting* research results. Science in general has far more to do with acts of interpretation than we generally like to acknowledge. If we were hoping to rely on science as a pure, objective enquiry into a pre-existing reality, this is troubling. Interpretation is neither pure nor objective. It is personal and perspectival. Scientists are people too. They have their own agendas and assumptions, prejudices and priorities. This is not to say that their perspectives are *bad*. On the contrary, scientists can be remarkably imaginative and creative. It just that the process doesn't exactly conform to our stereotypes of how "science" works.

As well as the interpretation of results, think of how much is done in the design of our next experiment, our next hypothesis – that is to say, by our capacities to imagine possibilities, to think in new directions, or to ask probing, unexpected questions. Such abilities might be more readily classified as *philosophical* than scientific. (Part of what I'm saying, I suppose, is that this distinction is a lot less robust than stereotypes of human enquiry would have us believe.)

We might think we can rely on science to know ourselves. But the "science of us" relies on self-reporting, interpretation, and asking the right questions. All of which relies on . . . our ability to know ourselves. So what are we really learning here? And this is not just a problem for happiness research. The same kind of circularity shows up all over the place, and not just in psychology – it affects some of the "harder" sciences too. How would we go about studying the neuroscience of romantic love? Let's say you want to run some fMRI scans on people who are in love. The thing is, first you have to *find* them. To distinguish them from your control group, you basically have to ask people to tell you whether they're in love or not. You're building foundational assumptions about people's ability to know themselves into your "scientific" method. Of course you could weed out the ones whose answers don't convince you, but then you're just replacing that set of foundational assumptions with some slightly different ones (about your *own* ability to know the hearts of others). It doesn't matter whether, once you've found your experimental group, you hand them a (subjective?) survey or put them in an (objective?) fMRI scanner. Trust in your subjects' self-reporting abilities, or in your own ability to tell if who's in love and who isn't, is by this point an essential part of your experimental design.[24]

On top of all that, the social sciences are experiencing what is often described as a "replication crisis" – profound challenges to the rigorous replicability of established results have thrown the field into a state of turmoil. This could, in the end, turn out to be a productive kind of turmoil. But right now it is a huge complication. Honestly, for this reason much of the social science research I have cited in this book has a small question mark hanging over it in my mind's eye. I still cite it, because I still want to use the best information available to me to make sense of the world. But I don't trust it unconditionally.

This doesn't mean that the science of us is useless, just that we should know it – and use it – for what it is. When it comes to love, in particular, I am a huge advocate for *more* and *better* science. Resisting scientific progress is part and parcel of the romantic mystification of love and the Romantic Mystique (mentioned in chapter 2). The science of love is a direct challenge to the Romantic Mystique. It would certainly be foolish to ignore the data and theoretical perspectives scientific research can offer.

But it would not be wise to assume that our deepest philosophical questions about love, happiness, and our own selves will generally be settled by scientists.

### If you're eudaimonic and you know it

If we can't even know something as relatively simple as whether we're *happy*, how on earth could we know whether we – and our loving relationships – are *eudaimonic*?

Eudaimonia as I imagine it is defined by "good spirits," and the "spirits" I have in mind exist and interact at every scale from the global to the personal. There's so much to consider: the state of your inner daimons, the vibe of the various communities you belong to, the time and place you live in, the spirit of your relationship itself . . . are all these daimons "good"? Knowing what's going on at all these different levels demands a high level of self-knowledge, and so much more besides.

But perhaps that isn't an insuperable problem. You might be eudaimonic and not know it. What matters more, I suggest, is that we *strive* for understanding – real understanding, with the rose-tinted specs off – of all these daimons around and within us. We work towards knowing ourselves and other daimons, accepting that this is always a work in progress rather than a completed task. And in the process of striving towards understanding, maybe we create the very things we seek to understand.

One way of explaining why it's so hard to "know ourselves" in the conventional sense is to say that there's *nothing there to know*. Long before meditation and mindfulness
were co-opted by mainstream positivity culture – before they
became a happiness-boosting form of "self-care" or a tool
for "self-improvement"[25] – some Buddhist traditions taught
these skills as a way of coming to understand that the "self"
as we now conceive of it *literally does not exist*.

For myself, I lean towards a more moderate thesis than
this: the self exists, but not as a pre-formed entity, sitting
around waiting to be known. It's more as if we are making
ourselves up as we go along. If that's the case, then admitting
we fundamentally don't *know* ourselves doesn't amount to
an admission of defeat so much as an acknowledgement that
one's very self is a work in progress. Not something fixed and
finished, but an ongoing story that we are in the process of
telling, with various narrative paths still open to us.

If you're thinking *whoa, that all sounds so existential . . .*
you're not wrong. I am borrowing a page from the existentialists' playbook here. Existentialism is a philosophical
movement that came into focus in the twentieth century
with the work of philosophers such as Jean-Paul Sartre and
Simone de Beauvoir. It's a multifaceted collection of ideas,
but for now I'm interested in one particular piece of it: this
idea that we make ourselves up as we go along or that, in
Sartre's famous phrase, "existence precedes essence."[26]

He means that we don't have a predetermined essence (or
nature). Rather, we simply exist, and then we *create* our own
natures through our decisions. We determine who and what
we are by making choices and taking action. As he puts it
in his famous 1946 lecture "Existentialism is a humanism":

What do we mean by saying that existence precedes
essence? We mean that man first of all exists, encounters
himself, surges up in the world – and defines himself
afterwards. If man as the existentialist sees him is not

definable, it is because to begin with he is nothing. He will not be anything until later, and then he will be what he makes of himself.

We don't have to conform to roles handed out to us by "nature," or by our "character," or by anything else. We can *pretend* we have to follow such pre-written scripts – such as the script for "woman" or "wife" – but this is a kind of abdication of responsibility, or what existentialists call "bad faith." To live an "authentic" life, they say, we must acknowledge that there really is no script, no essence, no premade "human nature." There's only what we do. What we choose. We're actually all playing massive choose-your-own-adventure games. Or so goes the classic existentialist line.

I, for example, don't have to conform to a pre-existing script for "womanhood" handed to me by "nature" – this is one major lesson of Simone de Beauvoir's existentialist feminism, as summarized in her famous slogan "one is not born, but rather becomes, woman."[27] For de Beauvoir, existentialism is in fact key to understanding the oppression of women. What that oppression consists in, she says, is the denial and undermining of women's agency, their authenticity, and so (by existentialism's lights) their full selfhood. Under patriarchy, women are positioned as "the other," as passive recipients of circumstance, rather than as whole persons or subjects in their own right.[28] De Beauvoir discusses how this plays out in the context of (hetero) romantic relationships in chapter 12 of her book *The Second Sex*. She argues that the situation places impossible demands on both men and women: women are expected to cede all their self-determination to a man, so they must position him as almost god-like in order to make this seem like a reasonable thing to do. But no man can live up to that kind of expectation. It doesn't end well. Of course, that was France in 1949. But, while some of the details have changed, we are still setting ourselves up to fail at "romance" by treating it as a predetermined script to which we must conform. We are still, in this sense, acting in "bad faith."

But if we take this point and abandon those scripts, are we *entirely* free to choose our own adventures? I'm not sure. As de Beauvoir explains, I'm not going to live a fully authentic life if I am *seen* (by myself and others) as limited by my essence – as confined to certain (e.g. womanly) roles. My authentic self can be constrained by others' perceptions of me just as much as my own bad faith.

I am sympathetic to this more refined take on existentialist authenticity. If anything, I would put even more emphasis on the role of others in the creation of the self. Contemporary philosopher Judith Butler[29] describes the performance of gender as "a practice of improvisation within a scene of constraint" and explains that

> one does not "do" one's gender alone. One is always "doing" with or for another, even if the other is only imaginary. What I call my "own" gender appears perhaps at times as something that I author or, indeed, own. But the terms that make up one's own gender are, from the start, outside oneself, beyond oneself in a sociality that has no single author . . .

I think something like this is how one performs (not only one's gender but) one's whole self. I might put it this way: I'm not *entirely* free to choose my own adventures, because these adventures are multi-player. While I may have no predetermined essence, nor am I the sole author of my own life story. There is a collaborative creation process going on: a collective co-authoring by (and *of*) myself and other daimons. In and through those collaborations, I can come to know myself and others, but I will never be *done* learning because the co-creation process is ongoing.

We will see, in the next chapter, how exactly the same thing might be true of loving relationships.

# 5
# Eudaimonic Love

## Love and "negative" emotions

When I was working on the material for this book, I was invited to present my research at a small group event near where I live. Over a pleasant dinner, I gave a short talk about romantic ideology, happiness, eudaimonia and philosophical ideas of the good life. And, afterwards, there was lots of time for Q&A and general discussion.

Dishearteningly, if predictably, attention quickly turned to my personal life, then homed in like a laser on the fact that I personally had two partners. For the rest of the evening, I fielded questions about sexually transmitted infections, jealous men, the ethics and legal ramifications of polygamy (being married to more than one person at once), and the somewhat intimate details of other guests' real and hypothetical relationship situations. I am not an expert on any of those subjects. I don't remember if anyone asked me about eudaimonia, or happiness, or romantic ideology. I do remember being told that my behaviour was immoral and that polyamory is the same thing as cheating.

Not everybody in the room got involved in the discussion. Some sat by and looked on. Some of them periodically said "hmm," or frowned or nodded at a comment or question. They acted as if this was a *normal* discussion. Appropriate treatment for a professional guest speaker.

I picked up the cues and played along. I nodded too. I said I was "happy to answer any questions." I was possessed by the spirit of the occasion, its daimon. We all acted as if it was normal for audience members at a philosophy talk to ask me about how I deal with STIs. And that is a self-fulfilling prophecy: we *made* it normal by treating it as such. If we had all acted as if it was weird and rude, it would have stopped right away. Toxic atmospheres are bad daimons that thrive under certain conditions: they remain strong and healthy as long as they are supported and sustained. The silence of onlookers is often exactly what such a daimon needs in order to thrive.

Eventually, someone did speak up. She pointed out that it was inappropriate to ask such intrusive and personal questions. But as soon she stopped talking, the conversation just closed up again around the disruption. It felt like watching living tissue heal itself. The daimon bounced back, as if nothing had happened. The *intervention* became the rude thing. Still, I appreciated the effort. And I appreciated hearing later, from another woman present, that she was not on board with the turn the evening took. As for the silent others, I wonder what was in their minds. Perhaps they silently wished me well. Their nods and smiles haunt me.

Some recent research[1] has looked into the effects of silently wishing other people well. In the study, participants were given this instruction: "As you walk around, I want you to notice the people you see. Really try to look at them and as you're looking at them, think to yourself, 'I wish for this person to be happy.' Try to really mean it when you think about it." The researchers found that doing this "resulted in lower anxiety, greater happiness, greater empathy, and higher feelings of caring and connectedness than the Control condition."

Two things strike me about this. First, the instruction to the subjects is all about what goes on inside their own minds. They aren't supposed to *say* anything to the people they see or *do* anything to make them happy. They are just supposed to wish them well and try to really mean it. Second, the positive effects of doing this that were measured in the study were all about the feelings of the well-wisher. The immediate effect of silently wishing others well is that it makes *you* feel better.

One might hope the practice would impact one's words and actions down the line, but that is by no means guaranteed. I recognize this in myself: I often witness injustice or suffering, and I often do not take action even though I could. Sometimes, despite not acting, I silently wish for the situation to improve. I wish the victims of injustice well. And I do, indeed, find that wishing so makes me feel a bit better. But that's precisely the source of my worry: by just wishing the victims well, I end up feeling better *without having to do anything*. What if that makes me less likely to actually do anything about the situation?

A relatively well-established psychological phenomenon known as "moral licensing" can manifest itself in exactly this way: feeling as if we have good intentions – that we have established our ethical credentials as it were – can make us more inclined to go on to do something morally dubious. Psychologists Anna Merritt, Daniel Effron and Benoît Monin explain:[2]

> Licensing can operate through an expression of the *intent* to be virtuous . . . Our framework suggests that when individuals have had a chance to establish their kindness, generosity, *or compassion*, they should worry less about engaging in behaviors that might appear to violate prosocial norms. For example, individuals whose past good deeds are fresh in their mind may feel less compelled to give to charity than individuals without such comforting recollections. (Emphasis added)

Sometimes, being a good daimon means speaking up to disrupt a toxic atmosphere. Speaking up in those situations usually doesn't feel nice. At least, not to me. It doesn't make me happier, and it certainly doesn't relieve my anxiety. Silently wishing someone well – thus establishing my own good intentions and strengthening my sense of myself as a compassionate person – *might* make me feel better. It might also make me act worse.

In this book I have not so far been speaking of eudaimonia as an individualistic phenomenon, rather intentionally shifting my emphasis from individuals to communities and networks, atmospheres and ecosystems. But daimons come in all sizes, from the very small (little daimons inside our own heads) to the globally huge (the patriarchy). *Being* a good daimon is also part of eudaimonia, and that specific aspect of eudaimonia is an individual phenomenon. Still, being a good daimon is not the subject matter of positive psychology. Being a good daimon is not defined by "positive emotions," feeling good or being happy. It may even be negatively correlated with those things, under certain circumstances.

Likewise as we wean ourselves away from the romantic conception of love and its happy ever after ideology, we can begin to see how deeply, disturbingly, *off-base* it is to think of love as happiness or as any kind of "positive" emotion. "Negative" feelings, such as sadness and anger, can be very important parts of love.

Let's consider anger as an example. (I'll come back to sadness in a moment.) As contemporary philosopher Myisha Cherry has powerfully argued,[3] anger exists for a reason. It is there to protect us in all arenas, from the intimately personal to the global and political. Instead of passively accepting harms done to ourselves or others, anger motivates us to do something about it. If someone acts wrongly towards my partner, the anger I feel about that is a protective measure: it prompts me to stand up for my partner, to try and ensure they are treated better in the future. To protect this member of my collaborative team. It prompts me to *be a good daimon* to my partner, and that is a key element of eudaimonic love. And in so doing I protect the meaningful *projects* I share with them, which constitute another defining feature of eudaimonic love.

But what about if it's my partner acting wrongly (towards me or someone else) and I feel angry about that? This too can be part of the experience of loving them. Myisha Cherry puts the point perfectly: "I cannot love you and let you get away with stuff."[4] In terms of my theoretical approach, my anger at you in these circumstances prompts me to help you be a better daimon, and that can be part of eudaimonic love too.

Anger doesn't feel nice. It's not a positive emotion or a happy state. Anger is excluded from the picture in "happy ever after" love. But it absolutely can be a part of eudaimonia, and of eudaimonic love. Eudaimonic love is not defined by any emotion, "negative" or "positive." Instead, it includes the full range of human emotion within its scope. All emotions have their role in a good-spirited life and in a good-spirited relationship.

In fact, the role of emotions such as anger is crucially important for understanding eudaimonic love because, although eudaimonic love does not center happiness, it's absolutely not about *ignoring* our feelings, or *sacrificing* our feelings, or enduring abuse from others. Anger is a defense against harm, including harm to or from someone we love, and eudaimonic love allows this defense mechanism to do its work by making space for "negative" emotions.

I want to draw out the contrast here with romantic love. On the romantic stereotype, we are supposed to stay with our "soulmate" for ever, whatever they do to us and whoever they turn into. The only fully acceptable way for a relationship to end is for one of the partners to die. This is a dangerous thing to believe, and not just because it might actively damage the relationship.[5] We are primed by romantic myths to think that any relationship that ends is a "failed" relationship. And nobody likes to fail.

As counterweight, let's consider another poet. Edna St Vincent Millay's "Passer Mortuus Est" concludes:

After all, my erstwhile dear,
My no longer cherished,
Need we say it was not love,
Now that love is perished?

Millay was pointing out, early in the twentieth century, that the end of a relationship doesn't have to mean that the love wasn't *real*. Unfortunately, most of us are still struggling to catch up with her a century later.

In the romantic love story, "happy ever after" is already the end of the story – there is no more to tell once the fated couple are united – whereas in eudaimonic love we have the freedom to make up our own love stories as we live them, and that includes the endings. Eudaimonic love doesn't prohibit certain emotions. It lets us be sad. It lets us be angry. And, crucially, if and when the time comes, it lets us walk away.

How would one know it's time to end things? Not necessarily by checking whether one's happy all the time. But maybe by realizing that one's deepest and most important life goals are better served by working with other collaborators. Identifying our most meaningful projects, whatever they might be – child-rearing, gardening, inventing rockets – can help us understand what gives our lives meaning, and that can help us understand who around us is a collaborator in those projects and who is not. Our emotions – all of them – can be guides in this respect.

As such, our emotions can work in tandem with our rational thought processes. The two are positioned as natural enemies by Romanticism, which emphasizes – through such poetic ambassadors as e e cummings – that "feeling is first" and "kisses are a better fate than wisdom." But we don't have to accept this. In my experience, when we pay close and loving attention to both, emotion and rationality can pull us together rather than apart. Eudaimonic love is not defined through opposition to rationality, as romantic love so often (and so problematically) is.

## Production and consumption

Making room for the "negative" emotions in eudaimonic love is part of waking up from the Emotional Dream I described back in chapter 1: the emotional analogue of the American Dream, which tells us that everyone can and should achieve self-made "emotional success" (i.e. happiness or positivity). The exclusion and deprecation of negativity is part of why the Emotional Dream – like the original American Dream – is a socially conservative force: all too often, when we shame people for being "angry" and "negative," we are systematically shaming the oppressed, the appropriately miserable, and the righteously pissed off. We are stifling critique and ignoring the need for change.

That's why respecting negative emotions can be a radical thing to do. More generally, moving away from the Romantic ideology of love has radical social potential. Capitalism depends on its constitutive American Dreams to keep us all focused on the pursuit of happiness and spending money in that pursuit. We are primed to think of ourselves as consumers and to think of "coupling up" as forming a new unit of consumption: you and your partner sharing a mortgage, buying groceries together, running a joint bank account.

I think this might be the key to understanding the idea that love is passive – that it's all about *feeling* something rather than *doing* something. We can turn to an economist of sex and love, Marina Adshade, for more clues about how this works. As she explains in an interview for my podcast *Labels of Love*,[6] "marriage is not what it used to be": we have collectively changed our minds about what the *point* is of coming together with someone in a marriage-like relationship.[7]

A marriage, Adshade says, was historically thought of as forming a unit of production. In marrying, a man and a woman were supposed to come together to collaborate in producing sustenance (for the average person) or wealth (for the historical equivalent of the 1 percent), as well as producing children. A marriage was construed as a very small firm, with each partner's contribution being determined by gender: the man would be responsible for economic productivity, while the woman took point on biological (re)productivity. A person's desirability as a marriage partner thus depended on their capacity to be productive according to their assigned gender role.

By contrast, as Adshade explains it, a marriage or comparable romantic partnership is now seen as a unit of consumption. Under capitalism, where individuals are consumers, a couple (and, by extension, a nuclear family) is simply a slightly larger consuming unit. Correspondingly, these days one might be expected to choose a partner on the basis of complementary tastes in whatever the couple might consume together (music, films, travel, or whatever else). Their "compatibility" is then framed in terms of consumer preferences rather than (re)productive potential.

This, of course, is not to say that men are no longer interested in fertile women and women are no longer interested in economically promising men. But such motives are no longer broadly socially acceptable as the primary motives for selecting a partner. Our narratives about who makes a good "match" have changed. Under Romantic ideology, a couple are supposed to marry (or enter into a marriage-like relationship) for *love* and nothing else.

In this role as match-maker, love gives rise to a new passive, consuming unit, not an active, producing unit. And so it makes sense that love will be seen as something that's more about how you feel when you're with another person rather than what you might be able to create in collaboration with them.

The idea that romantic attachments should be formed on the basis of (romantic) love and nothing else is strongly related to the good old "received wisdom" that I have been using to frame the discussion in this book. One more time, here's what it says:

1 A good life is one full of love and happiness. A bad life is one with neither.

2 Love and happiness (the best things in life) are "free."

3 In order to live a good life, one should *pursue* love and happiness (as opposed to crass things such as wealth, power, or fame).

The role of message #2 in this triad is essential – the Emotional Dream says that anyone can "make it" emotionally if they try. If happiness is "free," then it is, indeed, available to anybody. Or at least to anybody who deserves it – who doesn't just sit around whining about how sad and angry they are but instead knuckles down and does the gratitude journaling or the yoga classes or whatever else it takes for them to *earn* and *deserve* happiness.

I had a few things to say about message #2 back in chapter 1, insofar as the naïve idea that happiness is "free" ignores the (empirically confirmed) reality that poverty comes with some rather obvious *barriers* to happiness, while studies suggest that spending money (in particular ways) can actively promote it. But – a Romantic might be thinking here – at least we know money can't buy *love*. That's still sacred, right?

Hardly. Once we lay down the rose-tinted specs, romantic love appears to be subject to some pretty obvious socio-economic barriers: if you can't afford dinner and a movie, what do you do when your Tinder match suggests precisely that as a safe (public) first date? How do you "get out there and meet new people" when you don't have a lot of spare time to hang out at bars and clubs, sign up for a class, find some new hobbies, or join local groups for folks with similar interests?

If and when you do find somebody and enter into a relationship, economic hardship presents additional stressors that affect the *maintenance* of that relationship. A 2002 briefing paper on marriage and poverty in the USA, compiled by historian Stephanie Coontz and economist Nancy

Folbre,[8] offers a good summary of the research, indicating that "Unemployment, low wages, and poverty discourage family formation and erode family stability, making it less likely that individuals will marry in the first place and more likely that their marriages will deteriorate ... Poverty is a cause as well as a consequence of non-marriage and of marital disruption." These factors, naturally, impact people's choices when it comes to choosing who to meet, at least when seeking viable long-term partners:

> [I]ndividuals tend to seek potential spouses who have good earnings potential and to avoid marriage when they do not feel they or their potential mates can comfortably support a family. Ethnographic research shows that low-income women see economic stability on the part of a prospective partner as a necessary precondition for marriage. Not surprisingly, men increasingly use the same calculus. Rather than looking for someone they can "rescue" from poverty, employed men are much more likely to marry women who themselves have good employment prospects.
>
> Poor mothers who lack a high school degree and any regular employment history are not likely to fare very well in the so-called "marriage market." ... A study of the National Longitudinal Survey of Youth confirms that poor women, whatever their age, and regardless of whether or not they are or have ever been on welfare, are less likely to marry than women who are not poor. Among poor women, those who do not have jobs are less likely to marry than those who do ...

Income, in other words, can have rather *obvious* impacts on one's romantic prospects, interacting with other dimensions of "attractiveness."

And this is not just about who marries whom but also about people's willingness even to *date*. In her book *Dollars and Sex*, Marina Adshade includes an entire section called

"Money can buy you love," where she discusses a study in which women were asked how much a "seriously unattractive" man would have to earn in order for them to prefer to date him over a very attractive man. The answer is that the "seriously unattractive" guy would have to earn about $186,000 (US dollars) more than the really hot guy in order for a woman to prefer him. And we'd have to increase that considerably now to compensate for inflation – the data used here were gathered in 2003.[9] A pretty hefty price tag to buy back a woman's willingness to date you if you're "seriously unattractive." But my point is that there *is* a price tag on this.

When people are straight up admitting they won't date certain men unless they are very wealthy, it's not easy to maintain that love is "free" in anything like the idealistic sense. Of course, the question of what exactly counts as "love" in these contexts is fraught, but someone being willing to date you in the first place is both a pretty important starting point and a pretty important way in which certain people are selected out of the potential love match pool. A real kicker, to my mind, is that this phenomenon is gendered. The same studies found *no* corresponding price that the men were willing to pay to date a very unattractive woman. What this suggests to my mind is that the deep (and awful) answer to the question of whether money can buy love might be: it depends on who's being bought.

To properly understand the conceptual intricacies at stake in conversations about "buying love," we also need to think and talk – much more than we are currently supposed to do in polite company – about sex work. In particular, we need to think clearly about those situations where such work could be accurately characterized as *intimacy* work. The client who "just wants to cuddle" and talk about his marital problems is a cliché because he's real. The "girlfriend experience" is a real thing that is available in exchange for money. But what exactly is being purchased in such transactions? Not *love*, we might want to say. Still, the skilled provision of some of love's most important *aspects* or *ingredients* – such things as intimacy, care, and taking the time to really hear someone – these are all things that money can, and regularly does, buy.

Where does the "experience" end and "real" love begin? That is a complex question.[10] In our consumerist culture, where emotional labour of all kinds is available for purchase, and where wealth is very obviously (often *blatantly*) a factor in "private" romantic relationships, questions about how to manage the boundaries of commercial vs. personal intimacy become complex. If you feel as if sex work is peripheral to normal life (it isn't), bear in mind that there are also all kinds of other contexts in which intimacy – of both emotional and physical varieties – can be purchased. In the offices of psychological counsellors, registered massage therapists, and aestheticians, for example, the exchange of money for intimate services is deemed "respectable" but is in other ways quite similar. And, until the middle of the twentieth century, it was not unusual for a wealthy British woman to live or travel with a paid "companion" – not a servant, but a woman of comparable status lacking other financial support. A companion might provide some general assistance to her employer, but often her role was simply to be (in effect) a paid friend.

While we might find it comfortable to imagine "real" relationships and "real" love as clearly and cleanly separate from questions about who is buying what from whom, the realities of our socio-economic world make such a distinction feel a little naïve. And this makes perfect sense given that the deep social function of romantic love under capitalism is to take two individual consumers and forge from them a new, slightly larger, consuming unit. If you bring *money* to the partnership, the new unit will be able to afford to buy more stuff.

## Buy or build

Let's bring these thoughts about whether love is really "free" back into the context of the Emotional Dream. As I sketched it out in chapter 1, this version of the Dream consists in the idea that anyone can "succeed" emotionally – that is, live a life full of love and happiness – provided that they do the right things in their *pursuit* of an emotionally successful life. Love and happiness are there for the taking, the Dream says, provided you are willing to knuckle under and (as it were) pull your emotional socks up. I mentioned how readily "positivity culture" turns toxic when it starts to be about blaming individuals for their own lack of happiness (they are not sufficiently grateful, they are not meditating enough, etc.).

We can now see how the exact same patterns play out in the arena of romance. If we find ourselves "failing" in our love lives, there's always a long list of personal failures we can identify as the source of the problem. If we're unable to attract a partner, maybe we're not "putting ourselves out there" enough, or maybe we're "being too picky." Maybe we're just not "working on ourselves" enough. On the other hand, if we're in a relationship that we're not completely satisfied with, maybe we're not expressing our needs adequately, or maybe we're not doing enough to initiate regular sex, or maybe we're not prioritizing the other person. There's always *something* we could be failing to do. Popular culture is always standing by with copious "relationship advice" to help us pin down exactly what it is and exactly how we're failing to do it.

The "emotionally successful" person should be hashtag-blessed with a loving marriage and family. If you truly *deserve* it, love is meant to show up in your life. Think about the phrase "I can't believe you're still single!" That's meant to be a compliment, right? But *why* would it be complimentary? Because what you're trying to say is that the recipient is such a nice, attractive, and generally good person that it's incredible that love hasn't yet arrived for them. But that makes sense only if you think of love as a *reward* that they've earned and that life should have provided them with by now. Like something Santa brings if you've been good all year.[11] When you stop and think about it, it's actually quite strange to consider that a loving relationship with another person could ever be something you deserve or have earned. The other human being involved in such a relationship is presumably an autonomous agent with their own free will, not a prize you get for being a good person.

Looking at the bigger picture, one of the most important ideological roles of the Emotional Dream is to make us think about love and happiness at the level of individuals. This works in two ways. First, love and happiness are taken to be feelings – or positive emotions – which are things that an individual can experience. And, second, each of us is framed as being individually responsible for how much love and happiness we end up with.

This focus on individuals, their feelings and their just deserts acts as a deflector shield for awkward questions about the influence of structural issues such as racism or poverty. In the case of love, we are primed to ignore issues such as who has what kind of access to the dating "market" or to the kinds of social support that make a romantic relationship sustainable over time. And, once again, the hidden effect of all this is small "c" conservative. If we aren't even *thinking* about the role of social context in determining our emotional state, we won't be motivated to work towards any kind of social change in this connection. Indeed, we are primed to believe that love is eternal, "natural" and inevitable. That it "conquers all," that barriers of class and wealth crumble in the face of its mystical, magical influence. That's what the fairy tales say.

I also want draw in some of the theoretical background from my previous book, *What Love Is*, where I suggested that it actually "takes a village" to fall in love. For sure, romantic love is partly an evolved biological phenomenon that can usefully be located at the individual level (with a species-level history). But romantic love is also part social construct. Romance is *intensely* influenced by our social ideals and expectations, which give us a ready-made structure – a kind of script – for a romantic relationship. (In essence, the script is simply the playground rhyme: X and Y sitting in a tree . . . and you know the rest.) The effect of this scripting is that we are conditioned to expect, and also to want, that specific kind of relationship. So when we experience the powerful biological phenomena that come with romantic love, we are trained by social influence to *channel* that power in a particular direction, towards a permanent, monogamous, exclusive, nuclear-family-forming, "happy ever after" relationship. Such a relationship is considered "normal" (though it would be better described as "normative," as it is far from statistically normal). In *What Love Is*, I talked about romantic love being a process or function that takes adult desires and passions as its inputs, and then outputs nuclear families.

This is why I call attention to Adshade's economic point that marriage has become a force for generating consuming units rather than producing units. Nuclear families operate under capitalism as consumers. Slightly larger consumers than individual people, for sure, but structurally similar. Margaret Thatcher once said: "Society? There's no such thing! There are individual men and women and there are families."[12] Thatcher – like the big "C" (economic) Conservatism that she speaks for here – understands that "society" is a threat to capitalism, which requires a baseline of individuals operating selfishly in a competitive marketplace. Capitalism is destabilized by co-operatives, communities and collective action. Diverse and wide-ranging bonds of care that create and sustain such collectives are also a threat. But nuclear families are not. Nuclear families consume like individuals and can be set in competition against one another in the capitalist market.

Relationships that might encourage social co-operation beyond the nuclear family are risky to capitalism. Correspondingly, all caring relationships other than monogamous romantic couplehood are relegated to a secondary status, trivialized or criminalized. They are always treated as less-than: less intimate, less life-changing, less magical, less *real*, and less deserving of social or legal recognition. Looking under the hood at the mechanisms at work here, we can see that this is because such relationships, left to proliferate unchecked, could lead to the formation not of a new consuming unit but, rather, of a *society* in the sense that Thatcher couldn't abide.

There is an important connection between this piece of the machinery and Elizabeth Brake's concept of *amatonormativity*. I mentioned this briefly in my introduction: it's basically the idea that every normal (desirable) adult should be in romantic couple relationship and, moreover, their life should *center* around that relationship. Connections to (non-nuclear) family, or to friends, or to community, are all downgraded to that lesser status. We are pressured to focus all our most intense feelings of love and care *inwards* – symbolically, within the bounds of the nuclear family's iconic "picket fence." Research published in 2015, for example, finds that married people tend to have weaker ties to family, friends and neighbours than unmarried people.[13]

Viewed in a certain light, this makes us more manageable. For instance, it is harder for those dissatisfied with the way things are to *organize* at a community level once our community bonds have been weakened by this directing of attention inwards, towards the nuclear family, rather than outwards, towards wider social connections.

Historically, the nuclear family (along with the concordant "family values") has lain right at the heart of the political struggle between individualistic, conservative capitalism on the one side and collectivist, radical leftism on the other.

This goes back at least to Friedrich Engels, who attributed the nuclear family's very existence to capitalism, arguing that it benefited the bourgeoisie by ensuring their wealth would be retained through inheritance. Indeed, Engels tied conservatism to romantic monogamy very explicitly when he wrote in 1883: "It is a remarkable fact that with every great revolutionary movement the question of 'free love' comes to the fore."[14]

The debate still rages today, with David Brooks publishing a staunch critique of the nuclear family in left-leaning magazine *The Atlantic* in 2020,[15] prompting multiple incensed replies later the same year from the conservative think tank Institute for Family Studies.[16] Another conservative think tank, the Acton Institute, published a hilarious piece in 2019 about how socialists wish to abolish family dining.[17]

We don't talk about amatonormative pressure much, at least not explicitly. But it does its work best when it's *not* being talked about. It's as if we inhale it with the air, and this kind of almost invisible social pressure can be incredibly effective.

Writer and love researcher Mandy Len Catron is one of the people trying to push back against it. She uses research and reflection to make more informed decisions about how to live her own life:

When [my partner] and I talk about whether or not we want to get married, what we're really asking is how we want to define our sense of family and community. What is the role of care in our lives? Whom are we offering it to, and where are we finding it? I don't think choosing not to get married will save us from loneliness, but I think expanding our sense of what love looks like might. We've decided not to get married, for now, at least. I hope that might be a reminder to turn toward the people around us as often as we turn toward each other.

I find this really beautiful. I am married, but I still feel compelled to try and follow Mandy's example. Because I am polyamorous, and I do have other partners besides my husband, in a sense I have made a conscious decision to "turn towards" others as well as towards my spouse. But that in no way gives me a free pass here. Mandy's point is much more expansive and challenging than that. Including additional romantic partners in my life is still hewing pretty close to the romantic norm (for all it *seems* like a radical departure from certain angles). When I say I want to follow Mandy's example, I am talking in terms of my relationships with my friends, my extended family and my communities. How can I be better at turning my attention and care outwards in these directions? That is the question Mandy inspires me to ask of myself.

Conservative values, often flying under the banner of "family" values, encourage us to think of a romantic relationship as something wholly private. Something that goes on behind closed doors, away from public scrutiny, with which the public has no legitimate concern (except in the regulation, reinforcement and incentivization of marriage). They encourage us not to zoom out: to "pay no attention to the man behind the curtain," as it were. But, here as everywhere, *the personal is political.* This phrase – which is not attributable to any one particular author but emerged from the feminist movements of the 1960s – has long been a rallying cry to resist the kinds of nuclear family values that oppress women and maintain the traditional patriarchal order in "private" life, behind closed doors.[18]

But, in many ways, society at large has barely scratched the surface of what the phrase really means. We are especially slow when it comes to appreciating the impact of politics on our romantic relationships. Many of us now – finally – understand why it was necessary to intervene in politics to extend equal marriage rights to same-sex partners. But, with only a surface-level appreciation of what happened in that struggle, it would be all too easy to regard this one particular inequity as an exceptional situation – one that has now been dealt with – rather than merely one (particularly pointy) tip on a huge and deeply troubling iceberg. Until we appreciate that literally everything about romantic love is (at least) up for discussion, and that all kinds of real, substantive change are possible, we will not have learned the true lesson of 1960s feminism. That makes us depressingly slow learners.

One of the still underexamined root problems, I suspect, can be glimpsed at work in the idea of choosing between potential partners. The idea that one must *choose* a partner hearkens back to the discussion of "choice overload" in chapter 3. It is often opined that in the age of online dating we are made *less* satisfied, not more so, by the vast range of romantic prospects that are now (at least in theory) available to us. (Remember the "jam study," where people found it harder to choose any jam at all when there were several kinds on offer.) The problem boils down to this: there are always more profiles to swipe, more options to sample, so how can we ever feel fully satisfied with what we have? Any "choice" of a romantic partner induces anxiety about whether you've made the right choice. Whether *this* one is *the* one.[19]

That anxiety about whether one should "trade up" to someone else (someone better) strikes me as having deep roots in the conception of partners as *property*. In this sense, it shares its origins with the kinds of jealous, possessive feelings that can lead partners to restrict each other's freedoms – for example, their freedom to be friends, or even eat meals, with other people – and that, in the worst cases, can lead to violence or even murder. Historically, of course, men were the owners and women were their property. But simply extending the idea that partners are property to *all* partners is hardly the right way to level that playing field.

It is quite common, in everyday contexts as well as in scholarly research, to talk in terms of a "dating market" or a "romantic marketplace." Economic, and specifically capitalist, terms get applied to better understand (among other things) why certain partners count as more desirable, or more eligible, than others.[20] Why they are of "high value." It is also revealing, I think, that many recent philosophical theories of romantic love understand it in terms of a person's "value." Some say love is a response to *appreciating* someone's value – an "appraisal" of how especially valuable that person is – or that to love a person is to *assign* some value to them – a "bestowal" of special value.[21] I am not philosophically at home within this framework. The idea of one person having more or less "value" than others makes me uncomfortable. If a partner has a value, even if it is infinite, that means they can be *compared* in terms of value to other, less valuable, people. And that means, if they are not quite *property* any more, they can still be a status symbol. And a locus of status anxiety.

Partner-related status anxiety is not to be taken lightly. It can have dire consequences. As contemporary philosopher Kate Manne deftly explains in her recent book *Down Girl: The Logic of Misogyny*,[22] such anxiety fuels feelings of *inadequacy* in the eyes of the world which, when combined with the rage of frustrated men who feel entitled to a "desirable" or "high-value" female partner yet find themselves unable to attract one, can explode into acts of deadly violence and terrorism. This makes me feel unwell. But I don't mean to say it's a mistake – it strikes me as an important insight and descriptively accurate. What makes me feel unwell is the fact that *these are the right concepts* to describe how romantic love works.

What if, instead of thinking of partners as valuable objects to possess, we could conceptually reframe them in the way eudaimonic love demands: as collaborators, as co-creators? Might we be able to relieve some of our anxieties? In an intriguing way, doing this could amount to restoring one aspect of the old conception of marriage: a marriage was once a unit of production rather than a unit of consumption. Or a unit of shared activity rather than shared passivity. Perhaps there was something *to* that idea, something that has been lost in the era of romance. The romantic conception of love drives us to think of partners as co-consumers (or, in the worst case, as consumers *of each other*). But perhaps one day we might (again) understand the choice of a partner as being more about what we can build together than what we can buy together.

## Now what?

What to build? What to co-create with our loved ones? Art, children, communities, schools, science labs, inspiring lives of adventure, quiet lives of meditation . . . ?

Here we reach a point at which I can't help you. Eudaimonic love is not – it could never be – about *me* telling *you* what makes love (and life) meaningful. It's about you, and the people you (want to) love, figuring that out and working towards it together.

You get to change your mind at any time, though. Eudaimonic love is always a *work in progress*, just like a person is. Not something fixed and finished, but an ongoing story that we are in the process of telling, with many narrative paths still open to us. Back in chapter 3, I conjectured that eudaimonic love is not the "happy ever after" at the end of the story but, rather, the entire story. And telling the entire story of your love doesn't mean reading it out loud, as if it were a book that's already written: you are a co-author, helping to make the story up as you go along.

But wait – only a co-author? Why not *the* author? Because, as we saw back in chapter 4, your creative choices are always constrained. Not by some predetermined or fixed "essence" of who and what you are (at least, not if the existentialists are right), but by the circumstances you find yourself in and the daimons around you. We are, in a rather obvious way, only ever co-authors of our relationships: we co-create the story of the relationship *with another person or other people*. But that story is also constrained by external circumstances: time and place, social norms, political situations, family feuds, natural disasters, medical needs . . . anything can contribute to shaping a love story. Constraints are not necessarily negative, either: there can be something magical about the interplay of constraints and freedoms. After all, artists often use creative constraints as a strategic way to prompt their most interesting and original work.

The crucial thing, though, is that the existence of infinitely many constraints doesn't prevent you from being active within them. Just because you're not the sole author doesn't mean you are a passive *reader*. As the stories of our loves (and our lives) are written, constraints and freedoms are always present, albeit in constantly shifting configurations and in different proportions for different people. You are always and unavoidably a co-creator.

Another way of putting this is to say that eudaimonic love is *love with good spirits*, but that is a complicated, multidimensional thing. There are multiple interlocking and interacting daimons to consider, at different scales. Let me explain.

First, we can think about the individual people in the relationship. Are they good daimons? (To one another? To others?) Then, in addition to these, the relationship has its own daimon – its own spirit – and there's no guarantee that *it* will be good just because the people are good-spirited people. Some people, after all, are individually delightful but awful in an ensemble. (Ever had those two friends, both of whom you love dearly, who just can't be in the same room at the same time?) Then there are also all the external daimons around the relationship, making up the environment in which it must live and breathe. These form a complex ecosystem of daimons, big and small. For any love trying to grow within it, this ecosystem may function as a toxic atmosphere or as a life support system.

So eudaimonic love isn't the sort of thing we can assess with two settings (yes or no, on or off). It's a product of many factors. But what it is *not* about is happiness or happy ever afters, at least not in the contemporary sense. Contrary to romantic love, eudaimonic love is not defined by feelings at all. Eudaimonic love can involve powerful feelings, but they include all the "negative" ones such as anger and sadness, and they aren't what makes the love eudaimonic or what makes it "real" love.

Unlike romantic love, being sad is not a *failure* condition for eudaimonic love. Sad eudaimonic love also doesn't generally resemble the stereotypes of sad romantic love we looked at in the introduction (overblown, melodramatic, tragic and rather immature). There are better models for thinking about what sad eudaimonic love looks like. These could include the love of parents for their children in those times when child-rearing is intensely challenging and simply *doesn't feel good*, but is nonetheless deeply meaningful because it is one of the parents' core life projects.

It's intriguing that we are so much more ready to accept sad parental love than sad romantic love. Sad parental love is not generally seen as a failure, just as par for the course. In fact, we've *normalized* the idea that parents aren't going to have happy lives. But it doesn't have to be that way. It's been typical, at least since the 1970s, for parents to show up as being less happy than non-parents in studies. But, again, we mustn't underestimate the influence that large-scale socio-political daimons are constantly exerting on our personal loving relationships. This pattern is typical in the USA, where paid vacation is a rare luxury and childcare is very expensive. But in countries with plenty of paid vacation and inexpensive childcare, such as Norway and Finland, the gap is much smaller. In some cases, parents even show up as being happier than non-parents.[23]

In fact, the USA is by far the worst of twenty-two OECD countries recently compared in this regard, with a much bigger "happiness gap" between parents and non-parents than its next nearest rival (Ireland).[24] Actual "family values" – if they weren't just an ideological cover for conservatism – would motivate one to argue that paid time off work and access to inexpensive childcare are urgent priorities for the USA.

Another possible model for sad eudaimonic love could be found in grief. The passing away of a loved one does not end one's love for that person, but there is a process that is now part of the love, and that process does not feel good or consist in "positive" emotions. Nonetheless, grief is part of love. It's not a *failure* on behalf of the grieving individual but a necessary, healthy stage in loving the one who has died. It's no coincidence, I would argue, that recent philosophical and psychological research on grief is leaning in the direction of understanding how it relates to the loss and relearning of *meaning* in our lives.[25]

What sad parental love and grief have in common, and what sets both in stark contrast to the romantic stereotype of tragic sad love, is that they resemble more the greyscale grind of living with depression than the intense but short-lived pangs of an unrequited teen crush. If we want to understand how to love eudaimonically through sadness, there are much healthier models than Heathcliff.

Because eudaimonic love is less about feeling something and more about *doing* something, it is aligned with the tradition (which we looked at in chapter 3) from which bell hooks's vision of love emerges. In this (unromantic) tradition, love is active. It is not something that happens to us – something we "fall" into like a pit in the ground – but something we do. It is about making decisions and taking action. As I see things, eudaimonic love is about actively *crafting* our relationships to best suit the circumstances and the people involved and, through these relationships, *making* meaning, rather than passively waiting for happiness to arrive along with one's prince.

In turning attention from romantic feelings to the possibilities for meaningful collaboration, it is worth recalling that, back in chapter 3, we saw how making choices and taking action tends to make us feel better, whereas feeling helpless, passive and out of control are symptomatic of depression. Indeed, the entire Romantic Paradox is fueled by a feelings-first ideology of love that fosters passivity and disempowerment and is ultimately self-defeating. It's not surprising that this makes us *feel bad*. For this reason, practicing eudaimonic love might actually give us a better shot at happiness than the Romantic conception ever did, despite – or rather because of – the latter's focus on being "happy ever after" as life's central goal.

Bear in mind, though, that we can decline to make feelings definitive of love without denying that feelings are powerful and important. This is true of "negative" emotions just as much as "positive" ones – they can guide and motivate us in ways that can be crucial to our safety and survival. And, as I mentioned above, feelings are not the enemies of reason, whatever the Romantic ideology tells us. For what it's worth, this is my best guess as to what *wisdom* consists in: the smooth and seamless integration of rationality with emotion.

Because feelings aren't opposed to rationality, they don't relieve us of *responsibility* for our choices and actions. The idea that they do is traditionally another tool of Romantic patriarchy. This idea has played a role in denying agency to women – *how can they possibly be trusted with money and votes when they are so emotional and irrational?*; in justifying rape culture – *how can men possibly restrain themselves when overcome with miniskirt-induced lust?*; and even in men getting away with murder – *how can they be expected to refrain from killing "their" women when they are "overcome" with jealousy?*[26]

These ideas are garbage (if I may use a technical term), and it's time we took out the trash. The Romantic Mystique has a hand in sustaining them, promoting and glamorizing as it does a mass abdication of responsibility. *Love is out of control! Feelings! Passions! Total mystery! Not our fault! Move along, nothing to see here.* In existentialist terms, this attitude is one giant leap of bad faith, in the sense explained in chapter 4 above.

When we start to see love as active – as a collaborative, creative project rather than a set of feelings we passively experience – then we can appreciate that love is something we are responsible for. Just as the existentialists teach us that we are each, as individuals, responsible for the *person* we bring into existence through our individual decisions and actions, so an extended existentialism might reveal that in relationships with others we are, as a team of co-creators, jointly responsible for the *relationships* we bring into existence through our joint decisions and actions. We're not responsible for everything about those relationships, because our creative choices are always constrained. But we very certainly are responsible for what we choose within those constraints.

When I think about the relationship between myself and my husband, our own pattern of constraints and creative freedoms, it feels important that *we* – the team made up of Jonathan and myself – should not abdicate our responsibilities when it comes to the exercise of those freedoms. We shouldn't, as a team, act in *bad faith*. We could do so by pretending we have no choice but to conform to the societal script set up for us, the model of monogamy: marriage, mortgage, kids, grandkids, the exclusion of all others, until death do us part. While acknowledging that constraints are placed upon us by the cultural dominance of that model, we can and we must own the choices we are making every day in light of those constraints.

We chose to get married, for example, taking on all the social benefits and privileges that come with that status. We chose to be non-monogamous. And we chose to talk openly about being non-monogamous. How do I feel about each of those decisions, in retrospect? What about the decisions we'll make tomorrow, or next week, or next year? These aren't necessarily easy conversations to have with my conscience (or with my husband, although usually the former is worse). But they have to be had. Taking joint ownership of these choices we are making as a team is, I believe, a necessary part of eudaimonic love.

As we move forward together, I have started to see some changes afoot. Hints of a silver lining, perhaps, around the cloudy edges of the Zeitgeist. I see signs of a growing openness to understanding love as something active – something in which our choices can play a role – especially (although by no means exclusively) among younger people. This accompanies a growing sense of responsibility for the choices we make, not just in love but also in creating ourselves in other ways: as gendered individuals, for example.[27]

In a *New York Times* essay entitled "To fall in love with anyone, do this," Mandy Len Catron made famous the "36 questions" to accelerate intimacy with a potential partner. The essay instantly became a wildly popular viral sensation, which to me suggests that there is *huge* interest out there in the possibility of exercising our own agency where love is concerned. Catron, in an interview for my podcast *Labels of Love*, suggests that the phenomenon is related to technological change:[28]

The thing about online dating is that people have had to reckon with their ideas about fate. You start thinking, "I don't have to wait for this very serendipitous thing to happen to me, where there is a soulmate, and this person is brought to me through some sort of machinations of the universe . . ."

The realization is dawning – as online dating makes it impossible to ignore – that we have a lot more control, a lot more choice, and a lot more *responsibility* in this arena than the romantic mythology taught us to expect. This comes with upsides and downsides: It's both empowering *and* terrifying. The existentialists were preoccupied with how to deal with this terrible fact that we are responsible for our own choices – indeed, that we are at least to some degree responsible for creating ourselves through these choices. They addressed themselves to analyzing the "angst" – the nausea, in Sartre's terminology[29] – that this realization creates. No wonder existentialism feels like it's due for a comeback.

But just how silver are these silver linings? If we can all become more eudaimonic in our approaches to love and relationships, will that finally solve all our relationship problems? Will we then – at last – truly be happy ever after? Well, no. I hope that was the obvious answer, but, if it wasn't, please do not return this book to the store for a refund. (I don't think they give refunds for disappointing endings.) What I can offer as a consolation prize – and, genuinely, this consoles me somewhat – is the hope that you might experience your relationship as being *of higher quality* if it's eudaimonic. A 2016 study called "Finding meaning in us" reports findings that suggest people perceive their romantic relationships as being of higher quality when those relationships are also a source of meaning for them.[30]

Happiness just isn't where the action is in eudaimonic love. Whether or not you *feel* good, if you are able to practice eudaimonic love you will, by definition, be aligning your choices and your actions with your values and with what makes life meaningful to you. Not just you individually (though that is part of it), but also you collectively.

And, after all, was happiness ever the point of loving someone? That's not a rhetorical question. But only you can answer it.

I'll finish with a couple of small reflections on big subjects. Firstly: sad love isn't restricted to the love of a person. We can also experience sad love for a larger daimon, something that exists on a grander scale – sad love for a group of people, maybe, such as a family of origin. Or sad love for an institution such as a church or a university. Or even sad patriotic love of one's country.

I'm married to an American, and I've been watching a close-up, heartbreaking case study in sad patriotic love since the election of Donald Trump in 2016. I know many others have shared this experience of a cold awakening: coming to see, in a way no longer deniable or excusable, the moral depths to which a beloved country has been willing to sink. And I've been watching the dashed hopes of the #metoo movement, the disastrous leadership of Boris Johnson in Brexit Britain (my own country of origin), mass shootings in US schools, the constant betrayal of Indigenous peoples' rights to their lands and histories in what we call Canada (my adoptive home), overtly racist attacks on the rise more or less everywhere. And hovering above it all like a giant mushroom cloud, humanity's incapacity to save itself from imminent climate disaster.

It doesn't surprise me that I am *sad*. But, however sad I get, these days I find I can still get up in the morning and write. And that doesn't surprise me any more, either, because I remember the lesson of Viktor Frankl: if you can cultivate *meaning* in life, whatever that meaning might look like for you, that is enough. Having a purpose can keep you going even in the worst circumstances imaginable. My circumstances have never been anywhere near as bad as Frankl's, but in my limited experience the principle holds good.

I find that seemingly small things are enough to generate this effect for me – such as the thought that one day another person might read what I wrote and feel less alone. That kind of thought doesn't exactly make me *happy*. But being happy is not my life goal. It makes me feel my work is worth doing and ultimately makes me feel my life worth living. I even find a capacity for sad self-love through this work.

Secondly, if what I'm saying about reorienting ourselves towards eudaimonia sounds *scary*, in some deep but
difficult-to-articulate way, I get it. I feel like that too sometimes. Here is my best attempt to explain why. Eudaimonia
has little to do with the dominant ideologies of happiness
and romance. So there is something radical – and extremely
destabilizing – about suggesting that eudaimonia is a key for
understanding what it means to live a good life. It amounts
to dethroning happiness and disenchanting the romantic
dreams so many of us have held dear for much of our life-
times. That can be more than superficially uncomfortable.
These ideals can feel as if they *belong* to us, not merely
as peripheral or external influences but as fundamental,
life-structuring elements of our own psyches – part of who
we *are*. They can serve as fundamental pillars, too, for the
traditions and stories that create a sense of social or cultural
identity – that is to say, of who *we* are.

And so the threat of losing them can thus be (in quite a
literal sense) existentially scary. Turning away from romanticism towards eudaimonia may be philosophically promising, but it isn't safe. It feels as if we're sailing at night on a
troubled ocean, and I'm trying to turn out the lamps in all
the old lighthouses. And, to be fair, that is exactly what I'm
doing. But those beacons were guiding us onto the rocks.

# Notes

## Preface

1 Barbara Rosenwein provides an insightful commentary on some of love's constitutive fantasies in her book *Love: A History in Five Fantasies* (Cambridge: Polity, 2021).

2 *What Love Is And What it Could Be* (New York: Basic Books, 2017).

3 You can find a selection of them at www.carriejenkins.net/magazines and www.carriejenkins.net/radioandpodcasts.

4 I got hate *from* feminists – or at least from people who thought of themselves as feminists – for challenging the prevailing norm that all relationships should be monogamous. I had the impression that this critique came from people who had heard only that I was personally non-monogamous, and who weren't familiar with my critique of how the institution of compulsory monogamy sustains the patriarchal status quo.

5 These intersections of sexualized and gendered racism were less surprising to my partners.

6 Thi Nguyen offers an excellent description of this phenomenon in "Gamification and value capture," chapter 9 of his new book *Games: Agency as Art* (Oxford: Oxford University Press, 2020).

7 Recent work on this phenomenon includes Jin Kyun Lee's "The effects of social comparison orientation on psychological well-being in social networking sites: serial mediation of perceived social support and self-esteem," *Current Psychology* (2020), pp. 1–13, and Schmuck et al.'s "Looking up and feeling down: the influence of mobile

social networking site use on upward social comparison, self-esteem, and well-being of adult smartphone users," *Telematics and Informatics* 42 (2019), pp. 1–12.

8 See e.g. *Charles Darwin: Voyaging*, by E. Janet Brown (Princeton, NJ: Princeton University Press, 1996).

9 See "Newton, The Man," by John Maynard Keynes, https://mathshistory.st-andrews.ac.uk/Extras/Keynes_Newton/.

## Introduction

1 I don't think it works for mathematical rules, for example, although this was one of Wittgenstein's intended applications (as developed in his 1956 *Remarks on the Foundations of Mathematics*). In my 2008 monograph *Grounding Concepts: An Empirical Basis for Arithmetical Knowledge* (Oxford: Oxford University Press) I work from a very different conception of mathematics.

2 To call something socially constructed is not to deny its reality or its power. The process of constructing norms for love starts off with a rhyme and a fairy tale, but what we end up with is as real as a law, a church or a government (all of which are also social constructs – real and powerful ones). If love's rules are more vague and amorphous than those of these other constructs, that only helps love better evade scrutiny and challenge. We can't fight back against something if we can't even say what it is.

3 See Elizabeth Brake, *Minimizing Marriage: Marriage, Morality, and the Law* (Oxford: Oxford University Press, 2012), chapter 4.

4 For a recent and thorough scholarly exploration, see *Cultural Constructions of Identity: Meta-Ethnology and Theory*, ed. Luis Urrieta, Jr., and George W. Noblit (Oxford: Oxford University Press, 2018).

5 He didn't even invent the word "eudaimonia." And it might not have meant what he thought it meant. I'll say more about this later.

## Chapter 1 The Paradox of Happiness

1 One philosopher I don't get to talk with over dinner is John Locke. (He died in 1704.) It's widely hypothesized that in drafting the Declaration of Independence, and these words in particular, Thomas Jefferson was inspired by similar phrases in Locke's *Letter Concerning Toleration* and his *Essay Concerning Human Understanding*. Locke's opposition to the divine right of kings certainly made him an expedient philosopher for the moment, and his political philosophy notably positions the "pursuit of happiness" as the foundation of liberty itself.

2 Despite the gendered language of the book's standard English title, Frankl's discussion seems to be about humanity in general. Interestingly, the title was *not* gendered in the original German.

3 To read more of what James has to say about this, see his book *The Varieties of Religious Experience*, particularly lectures IV–VII.

4 This "law" was not invented, only expounded, by *The Secret*.

5 A summary of some relevant recent data is provided by CNN here: www.cnn.com/2021/06/01/politics/black-white-racial-wealth-gap/index.html.

6 Recent data on racialized dating preferences, collected by dating website OKCupid, is summarized by NPR here: www.npr.org/2018/01/09/575352051/least-desirable-how-racial-discrimination-plays-out-in-online-dating.

7 Famously, Trump's advisor Kellyanne Conway coined this phrase in 2017 in defense of false claims made by press secretary Sean Spicer about the size of Trump's inauguration crowd.

8 If you've seen *The Good Place*, you may know utilitarianism as the philosophical position to which Judith Jarvis Thompson's "Trolley Problem" was designed as an objection (Season 2, Episode 6).

9 John Stuart Mill, *Autobiography*, chapter 5.

10 Yulia Chentsova-Dutton et al., "And they all lived unhappily ever after: positive and negative emotions in American and Russian picture books," *Emotion* (advance online publication, 2021).

11 Philosopher Mike Martin has categorized a dozen different versions. See chapter 7 of his 2012 book, *Happiness and the Good Life* (Oxford: Oxford University Press).

12 Iris B. Mauss et al., "Can seeking happiness make people unhappy?" *Emotion* 11 (2011), pp. 807–15. In case you're wondering, the researchers do make efforts to check whether it is the higher valuation of happiness that causes lower levels of happiness (rather than the other way around) by inducing subjects to value happiness more. "To lead participants to value happiness," they say, "we used a fake newspaper article extolling the importance of happiness." They also "used film clips pretested to induce happiness or sadness" in order to "manipulate emotional context in a standardized fashion" and "rule out potential confounds such as positive emotional reactivity."

13 *The Methods of Ethics*, Book I, chapter 4. This wording comes from the seventh edition of 1907.

14 A recent study of this phenomenon found that "heterosexual men were most likely to say they usually-always orgasmed when sexually intimate (95%), followed by gay men (89%), bisexual men (88%), lesbian women (86%), bisexual women (66%), and heterosexual women (65%)." For more details, see David A. Frederick et al., "Differences in orgasm frequency among gay, lesbian, bisexual, and heterosexual men and women in a U.S. national sample," *Archives of Sexual Behaviour* 47 (2018), pp. 273–88.

15 "Yes, yes, yes: why female pleasure must be at the heart of sex education," November 13, 2018.

16 See for example *The Happiness Project* by Gretchen Rubin (New York: HarperCollins, 2009) or *The Happiness Equation* by Neil Pasricha (New York: G. P. Putnam's Sons, 2016).

17 The talk is from 2004, and can be viewed at www.ted.com/ talks/mihaly_csikszentmihalyi_flow_the_secret_to_happi ness.

18 "Relationship between wealth, income and personal well-being, July 2011 to June 2012," http://www.ons.gov.uk/ons/ dcp171776_415633.pdf.

19 See Betsey Stevenson and Justin Wolfers, "Subjective well-being and income: is there any evidence of satiation?" *American Economic Review: Papers and Proceedings* 103 (2013), pp. 598–604.

20 Julie Norem and Edward Chang, "The positive psychology of negative thinking," *Journal of Clinical Psychology* 58 (2002) pp. 993–1001.

21 Ashley Whillans et al., "Buying time promotes happiness," *Proceedings of the National Academy of Sciences of the United States of America* 114 (2017), pp. 8523–27.

22 The article can be read online at: www.theguardian.com/ commentisfree/2016/may/17/money-cant-buy-happi ness-wishful-thinking.

23 L. Parker Schiffer and Tomi-Ann Roberts, *Journal of Positive Psychology* 13 (2017), pp. 1–8.

24 Don't get me started on the equivalent situation with the word "love." It has multiple entries, each with its own sub-entries. One of them – and this was news to me – is "any one of a set of transverse beams supporting the spits in a smokehouse for curing herring."

25 Discussions of hap frame Sara Ahmed's book *The Promise of Happiness* (Chapel Hill, NC: Duke University Press, 2010), which I highly recommend to those interested in happiness and its ideological role.

26 See *Bright-Sided: How Positive Thinking is Undermining America* (New York: Metropolitan Books, 2009), in which she says, "[t]he real conservatism of positive psychology lies in its attachment to the status quo, with all its ine-qualities and abuses of power. Positive psychologists' tests of happiness and well-being, for example, rest heavily on

measures of personal contentment with things as they are" (p. 170).

27 *America the Anxious: How Our Pursuit of Happiness Is Cultivating a Nation of Nervous Wrecks* (New York: St Martin's Press, 2016).

28 In 2003, Robert Emmons and Michael McCullough published a study called "Counting blessings versus burdens: an experimental investigation of gratitude and subjective well-being in daily life" in *Journal of Personality and Social Psychology* 84 (pp. 377–89). They report that subjects in their gratitude condition "exhibited heightened well-being across several, though not all, of the outcome measures" and that "[t]he effect on positive affect appeared to be the most robust finding." More recently, Fuschia Sirois and Alex Wood published a paper titled "Gratitude uniquely predicts lower depression in chronic illness populations: a longitudinal study of inflammatory bowel disease and arthritis" in *Health Psychology* 36 (2017), pp. 122–32. Alex Wood et al.'s paper "Gratitude and well-being: a review and theoretical integration," *Clinical Psychology Review* 30 (2010), pp. 890–905, also discusses a range of earlier studies.

29 J. R. R. Tolkein, *The Two Towers: Being the Second Part of The Lord of the Rings* (London: George Allen & Unwin, 1954).

## Chapter 2 The Romantic Paradox

1 The phrase "your fave is problematic" derives from a Tumblr that was briefly popular in the mid 2010s: https://yourfaveisproblematic.tumblr.com/.

2 The term "benevolent sexism" was coined by Peter Glick and Susan Fiske in an article titled "The ambivalent sexism inventory: differentiating hostile and benevolent sexism," *Journal of Personality and Social Psychology* 70 (1996), pp. 491–512. A good definition is provided in

Glick et al.'s paper "Beyond prejudice as simple antipathy: hostile and benevolent sexism across cultures," *Journal of Personality and Social Psychology* 79 (2000), pp. 763–75: "a subjectively positive orientation of protection, idealization, and affection directed toward women that, like hostile sexism, serves to justify women's subordinate status to men."

3 For current purposes, I'm setting aside the question of whether cummings is being ironic. And the separate question of whether, even if he were, such putative irony would be generally appreciated by the poem's readers.

4 For more reflections on this, I recommend this entry of Mandy Len Catron's at her blog *The Love Story Project*: https://thelovestoryproject.ca/2013/09/12/im-willing-to-lie-about-how-we-met/.

5 I talk about some of the problems in the later chapters of *What Love Is*.

6 Justin Lehmiller and Christopher Agnew, "Marginalized relationships: the impact of social disapproval on romantic relationship commitment," *Personality and Social Psychology Bulletin* 32 (2006), pp. 40–51.

7 H. Sinclair et al., "Don't tell me who I can't love: a multimethod investigation of social network and reactance effects on romantic relationships," *Social Psychology Quarterly* 78 (2015), pp. 77–99.

8 Patterson's remarks can be found in a *Huffington Post* article, 28 May, 2017, www.huffpost.com/entry/how-repre sentation-worksor-doesnt_b_59179e37e4b00ccaae9ea3 9d (emphasis added). For more of his work on the intersections of race and polyamory, I recommend his book *Love's Not Color Blind* (Portland, OR: Thorntree Press, 2018).

9 This terminology is introduced in Miranda Fricker's book *Epistemic Injustice: Power and the Ethics of Knowing* (Oxford: Oxford University Press, 2007).

10 For recent discussion of this phenomenon, see Debra

Jackson, "'Me too': epistemic injustice and the struggle for recognition," *Feminist Philosophical Quarterly* 4 (2018), pp. 1–19.

11 See Terri Conley et al., "Investigation of consensually non-monogamous relationships: theories, methods, and new directions," *Perspectives on Psychological Science* 12 (2017), pp. 205–32. (Also, for reasons I'll discuss later in this book, I raise a sceptical eyebrow at the thought that scientists are the real experts here.)

12 For more on this particular absence, see writing professor Camilla Nelson's 2017 essay in *The Conversation* titled "From grotesques to frumps – a field guide to spinsters in English fiction," https://theconversation.com/friday-essay-from-grotesques-to-frumps-a-field-guide-to-spinsters-in-english-fiction-73680. Nelson surveys a range of spinster stereotypes and explains their cultural impact.

13 See, for example, Fisher's article "Love is like cocaine," published in *Nautilus* in 2016, http://nautil.us/issue/33/attraction/love-is-like-cocaine.

14 The name is deliberately chosen to parallel Betty Friedan's label for a similar bundles of attitudes applied to women; see her book *The Feminine Mystique* (New York: W. W. Norton, 1963).

15 See her book *Love and Limerence: The Experience of Being in Love* (New York: Stein & Day, 1979). Tennov includes sexual attraction as a component of limerence, but the reality of romantic asexual experience entails that this is incorrect.

16 In fact, the paper in which this scale was originally described ("Measuring passionate love in intimate relationships," by Elaine Hatfield and Susan Sprecher, *Journal of Adolescence* 9 (1986), pp. 383–410) even points out that others would call what is being measured here "a crush" or "infatuation."

17 In her doctoral dissertation, *The Syndrome of Romantic Love*, 2018, https://academicworks.cuny.edu/cgi/viewconte

nt.cgi?article=3884&context=gc_etds. The quoted passage appears on p. 31.

18 See chapter 7 of *What Love Is* for more on this.

19 Helen Fisher et al., "Intense, passionate, romantic love: a natural addiction? How the fields that investigate romance and substance abuse can inform each other," *Frontiers of Psychology* 7 (2016), pp. 1–10.

20 Some philosophers will be annoyed that I don't distinguish here between a "feeling" and an "emotion." Some of them might want me to say that "merely physical" feelings (such as pain or hunger) are not emotions. Some might want me to say that emotions involve aspects of *evaluation* or *motivation*, and not (just) feeling. I'll admit that I have some reservations about this distinction between feelings and emotions (especially about the idea that emotions are not "merely physical" the way pain and hunger are). In any case, the precise details of *how* to make the distinction are fraught, and there is no settled definition of either term. But, more importantly for current purposes, in everyday life – which is the source of the culturally dominant conceptions of love and happiness that interest me here – the two are so often treated as interchangeable that giving much weight to the distinction would be inappropriately artificial in this context.

21 See her paper "What good are positive emotions?" *Review of General Psychology* 2 (1998), pp. 300–19.

22 Specifically, Fredrickson says that "love experiences are made up of many positive emotions, including interest, joy and contentment."

23 "Framing love: when it hurts to think we were made for each other," *Journal of Experimental Social Psychology* 54 (2014), pp. 61–7.

24 I am grateful to my PhD student Chase Dority for conversations that substantively informed my thinking in this chapter.

### Chapter 3 Daimons

1 That said, there are some points where Aristotle's interests and mine converge – the role of *chance* in eudaimonia (putting the "hap" back in "happiness") is one such.

2 In one contemporary interpretation, your "daimon" is like a calling – something that guides you in accordance with your innate character, or soul. This soul is like an "acorn" inserted into a physical body – it determines, once and for all, the essence of who you are. This is James Hillman's view, as described in his book *The Soul's Code: In Search of Character and Calling* (New York: Random House, 2013). I mention this view here only to point out that, despite using the same word, "daimon," Hillman's views are, in a number of ways, antithetical to my own.

3 Summarizing in the *Stanford Encyclopedia of Philosophy*, Richard Kraut says: "Aristotle never calls attention to this etymology in his ethical writings, and it seems to have little influence on his thinking. He regards 'eudaimon' as a mere substitute for eu zên ('living well')." See https://plato.stanford.edu/entries/aristotle-ethics/ for more information.

4 A "glamour" originally meant a magic spell, especially one to make something appear more attractive than it really is. Here is Merriam-Webster on the history of the word: "It wasn't until the mid-1800s that the word glamour started to separate from its magical connotations – though those connotations weren't, and still aren't, entirely gone. Glamour in its modern senses – 'an exciting and often illusory and romantic attractiveness' and 'alluring or fascinating attraction' – still has a bit of magic to it, though not usually of the suspicious variety." I guess I remain suspicious. To read more, see www.merriam-webster.com/words-at-play/the-history-of-glamour.

5 It can be tempting to think that scientific panpsychists are very different from spiritual panpsychists: the scientist rounds human consciousness *down* to the level of a physical

system (for short, call this being "reductionist"), while the spiritualist rounds everything else *up* to the level of human consciousness (for short, call this being "woo"). But that's a misconception. If panpsychism is true, it moves nothing either up or down. In fact, these "upwards" and "downwards" directions (consciousness is "up," physical things are "down") do not correspond to any real dimension of difference, and that's supposed to be the point.

6 Sometimes, philosophers talk as if eudaimonia were a kind of happiness, just a different kind from hedonic (pleasure-based) happiness. We can talk that way – after all, we can talk however we want. But I don't think it's helpful, because it muddies the waters. The associations between happiness and feeling good are now so strong that it's impossible to ditch them. Frankl tried to help his fellow prisoners in the concentration camp by guiding them to find some meaning in their lives that would help them to survive. As I see things, he was helping them appreciate the ways in which their lives were still eudaimonic. But was he trying make them appreciate the ways in which their lives were still *happy*? That sounds wrong to me. Sometimes a word such as "happy" has to be left behind, even if a philosophical case could be made that it is technically applicable, because finding the right way of putting things is about more than technicalities.

7 For details, see his book *The Will to Meaning: Foundations and Applications of Logotherapy* (New York: World, 1969).

8 See, for example, Freud's *Civilization and its Discontents* (1930), where he writes: "what decides the purpose of life is simply the programme of the pleasure principle. This principle dominates the operation of the mental apparatus from the start."

9 Research on solitary confinement shows that it can have extremely serious adverse effects. See, for example, Jeffrey Metzner and Jamie Fellner, "Solitary confinement and mental illness in U.S. prisons: a challenge for medical

ethics," *Journal of the American Academy of Psychiatry and the Law* 38 (2010), pp. 104–8.

10 See Amy Novotney, "The risks of social isolation," *Monitor on Psychology* 50 (2019), www.apa.org/monitor/2019/05/ce-corner-isolation.

11 Aliya Alimujiang et al., "Association between life purpose and mortality among US adults older than 50 years," *Journal of the American Medical Association* 2 (2019), pp. 1–13.

12 Viktor Frankl, *Man's Search for Meaning* (London: Hodder & Stoughton, 1946).

13 She develops this idea in her book *all about love: new visions* (New York: William Morrow, 2000).

14 *The Art of Loving* (New York: Harper & Row, 1956).

15 *The Road Less Travelled* (New York: Simon & Schuster, 1978).

16 In his sermon "Loving your enemies," delivered at Dexter Avenue Baptist Church on 17 November 1957. The full text can be found at https://kinginstitute.stanford.edu/king-papers/documents/loving-your-enemies-sermon-delivered-dexter-avenue-baptist-church.

17 A summary of this approach can be found in section 3 of the *Stanford Encyclopedia of Philosophy* entry for "Love," https://plato.stanford.edu/entries/love/#LoveRobuConc.

18 This is something others have also noticed; bell hooks talks about it in the opening chapter of *all about love*.

19 "Crafting a job: re-envisioning employees as active crafters of their work," *Academy of Management Review* 26 (2001), pp. 179–201.

20 This description comes from a video presentation by Wrzesniewski, which can be viewed online at: www.youtube.com/watch?v=C_igfnctYjA.

21 Quotes in this paragraph are from the same presentation mentioned in note 20.

22 *The Upward Spiral: Using Neuroscience to Reverse the Course of Depression, One Small Change at a Time* (Oakland, CA: New Harbinger, 2015).

23 See, for example, the US National Institute of Mental Health symptom summary for depression: www.nimh.nih.gov/health/topics/depression/index.shtml.

24 From Justin M. Berg, Jane E. Dutton and Amy Wrzesniewski, "What is job crafting and why does it matter?," University of Michigan, 2007, http://positiveorgs.bus.umich.edu/wp-content/uploads/What-is-Job-Crafting-and-Why-Does-it-Matter1.pdf.

25 From Wrzesniewski et al., "Job crafting and cultivating positive meaning and identity in work," in A. B. Bakker (ed.), *Advances in Positive Organizational Psychology* (Bingley: Emerald, 2013, pp. 281–302).

26 Again, this wording comes from her presentation at www.youtube.com/watch?v=C_igfnctYjA.

27 See chapter 21.

28 Wrzesniewski discusses this possibility in the same video presentation mentioned previously.

29 "To stay in love, sign on the dotted line," www.nytimes.com/2017/06/23/style/modern-love-to-stay-in-love-sign-on-the-dotted-line-36-questions.html.

30 See her popular book *Mating in Captivity: Unlocking Erotic Intelligence* (New York: HarperCollins, 2006).

## Chapter 4 Know Thyself

1 Sheena Iyengar and Mark Lepper, "When choice is demotivating: can one desire too much of a good thing?" *Journal of Personality and Social Psychology* 79 (2000), pp. 995–1006.

2 The appeal of trusted curators or editors to limit the range of options available is as noticeable to me when I'm shopping as it is when I'm consuming online content.

3 Jamie Ducharme, "How to use dating apps without hurting your mental health, according to experts," *Time*, 16 August 2018, https://time.com/5356756/dating-apps-mental-health/.

4 Alexander Chernev et al., "Choice overload: a conceptual review and meta-analysis," *Journal of Consumer Psychology* 25 (2015), pp. 333–58.

5 A caveat: the jam study and the 2015 follow-up were specifically investigating *consumer* choice, not romantic choice. That said, contemporary attitudes to romance are in many ways reminiscent of capitalistic attitudes to purchase and ownership (see my book *What Love Is*, pp. 136–7, 160–2, and 172 for more on how problematic this is). So the analogy may be closer than it looks.

6 A full resolution of this scenario involves questioning the idea that humans can always be ranked as "better than" or "worse than" one another. Some people are simply incomparable, and attempting to rank them is a foolish exercise.

7 See Barry Schwartz et al., "Maximizing versus satisficing: happiness is a matter of choice," *Journal of Personality and Social Psychology* 83 (2002), pp. 1178–97.

8 Roy F. Baumeister et al., "Some key differences between a happy life and a meaningful life," in *Journal of Positive Psychology* 8 (2013), pp. 505–16. An intriguing range of other differences between "happiness" and "meaningfulness" is also suggested in this research:

> Satisfying one's needs and wants increased happiness but was largely irrelevant to meaningfulness. Happiness was largely present oriented, whereas meaningfulness involves integrating past, present, and future. For example, thinking about future and past was associated with high meaningfulness but low happiness. ... Higher levels of worry, stress, and anxiety were linked to higher meaningfulness but lower happiness. Concerns with personal identity and expressing the self contributed to meaning but not happiness.

9 For those unfamiliar with cognitive biases, the podcast *Philosophy Talk* offers an accessible introduction here: www.philosophytalk.org/shows/cognitive-bias.

10 See Vera Hoorens, "Self-enhancement and superiority biases in social comparison," *European Review of Social Psychology* 4 (2011), pp. 113–39, and especially the research summarized in the section "Illusory superiority."

11 The thesis was first put forward by Lauren Alloy and Lyn Yvonne Abramson in their paper "Judgment of contingency in depressed and nondepressed students: sadder but wiser?" *Journal of Experimental Psychology: General* 108 (1979), pp. 441–85.

12 "Depressive realism," *Aeon* (2020): https://aeon.co/essays/ the-voice-of-sadness-is-censored-as-sick-what-if-its-sane.

13 Of course, this is not to say that all sad love is eudaimonic.

14 Freud's book *The Interpretation of Dreams*, originally published in 1899, has been hugely influential in this regard.

15 This is from their book *Happy Money: The New Science of Smarter Spending* (New York: Simon & Schuster, 2013).

16 A good place to start, if you're interested in why they would say this, is Brie Gertler's entry on self-knowledge in the *Stanford Encyclopedia of Philosophy*: https://plato.stanford. edu/entries/self-knowledge, particularly §1.1.

17 His *Meditations*, first published in 1641, are the source of these ideas.

18 The earliest attribution is to Pierre Gassendi. Details can be found in Saul Fisher's entry on Gassendi in the *Stanford Encyclopedia of Philosophy*: https://plato.stanford.edu/ entries/gassendi/.

19 See www.pewsocialtrends.org/2006/02/13/are-we-happy-yet.

20 Jaime Napier and John Jost, "Why are conservatives happier than liberals?" *Psychological Science* 19 (2008), pp. 565–72.

21 Sean Wojcik et al., "Conservatives report, but liberals display, greater happiness," *Science* 347 (2015), pp. 1243–6.

22 These stereotypes can be dangerous, too: serious mental illness will fly below the radar if we don't know what it *really* looks like, going unnoticed until it's too late. Assuming we can tell how others feel based on whether they are smiling

in their photographs and using positive vocabulary could turn out to be a life-and-death level mistake. The UK charity Time to Change runs a campaign addressing the headclutcher stereotype. It's called "Get the Picture" and has the tagline: "people with mental health problems don't look depressed all the time."

23 Daniel Kahneman and Alan Krueger, "Developments in the measurement of subjective well-being," *Journal of Economic Perspectives* 20 (2006), pp. 3–24.

24 I wrote about this issue in more detail in my paper "Knowing our own hearts: self-reporting and the science of love," *Philosophical Issues* 26 (2016), pp. 226–42.

25 For more on this, see Ronald Purser, *McMindfulness: How Mindfulness Became the New Capitalist Spirituality* (New York: Random House, 2019).

26 An accessible overview of the implications of this idea can be found in in the *Stanford Encyclopedia of Philosophy* entry on "Existentialism" by Steven Crowell: https://plato.stanford.edu/entries/existentialism.

27 See her 1949 book *The Second Sex* for a full treatment.

28 Although de Beauvoir is focused on gender, the same pattern of "othering" can also manifest in many other domains.

29 In her book *Undoing Gender* (London: Routledge, 2004).

## Chapter 5  Eudaimonic Love

1 Douglas Gentile et al., "Caring for others cares for the self: an experimental test of brief downward social comparison, loving-kindness, and interconnectedness contemplations," *Journal of Happiness Studies* 21 (2020), pp. 765–78.

2 Anna C. Merritt et al., "Moral self-licensing: when being good frees us to be bad," *Social and Personality Psychology Compass* 4 (2010), pp. 344–57.

3 See for example her article "Anger can build a better world," *The Atlantic*, 25 August 2020, www.theatlantic.com/ideas/archive/2020/08/how-anger-can-build-better-world/615625/.

4 This quote is from her interview for my podcast *Labels of Love*, which can be downloaded at www.carriejenkins.net/podcast/2017/10/23/season-1-episode-7-politics. Her book *The Case for Rage* (New York: Oxford University Press, 2021) treats this topic in much more depth.

5 We saw, back in chapter 2, how some research suggests it may harm a relationship to think of it as a perfect, pre-destined unity rather than a shared journey, and how the soulmate myth frames single people as defective.

6 The episode can be downloaded at www.carriejenkins.net/podcast/2017/9/15/season-1-episode-6-money.

7 See also her 2017 article "Sexbot-induced social change: an economic perspective," in John Danaher and Neil McArthur (eds), *Robot Sex: Social and Ethical Implications* (Cambridge, MA: MIT Press, 2017).

8 The paper can be read in full at: www.pbs.org/wgbh/pages/frontline/shows/marriage/etc/poverty.html.

9 Günther Hitsch, Ali Hortacsu and Dan Ariely, "What makes you click? Mate preferences and matching outcomes in online dating," MIT Sloan Research Paper No. 4603-06, cited on p. 75 of Adshade's *Dollars and Sex* (Toronto: HarperCollins, 2013). A later version of this paper was published in *Quantitative Marketing and Economics* 8 (2010), pp. 393–427. The 2010 version omits the result describing this $186,000 compensatory price tag. In personal communication, however, Professor Ariely has confirmed that the result was robust, and it was omitted only because it struck the authors as rather an esoteric way of expressing their data.

10 For one recent discussion of these complexities, see María Gómez Garrido's "Being like your girlfriend: authenticity and the shifting borders of intimacy in sex work," *Sociology* 52 (2018), pp. 384–99.

11 There are also other reasons why this phrase is not an ideal compliment in most circumstances. Its underlying message is that a good person *should* be in a relationship, hence

it's surprising if they're not. Think about it for a minute and you'll see how what you're saying is that *being single is something that's meant to happen only to the bad people*. Like a kind of punishment. And that's simply not true – some people choose to be single, and it doesn't mean there's anything wrong with them.

12 This quote comes from an interview for the magazine *Woman's Own* in 1987, transcribed here: www.margaret thatcher.org/document/106689.

13 Natalia Sarkisian and Naomi Gerstel, "Does singlehood isolate or integrate? Examining the link between marital status and ties to kin, friends, and neighbors," *Journal of Social and Personal Relationships* 33 (2016), pp. 361–84.

14 In *Das Buch Der Offenbarung*; my translation.

15 See www.theatlantic.com/magazine/archive/2020/03/the-nu clear-family-was-a-mistake/605536.

16 See e.g. https://ifstudies.org/blog/yes-david-brooks-the-nu clear-family-is-the-worst-family-form-except-for-all-others.

17 See www.acton.org/publications/transatlantic/2019/12/02/ enjoy-your-family-thanksgiving-socialism-would-abolish-it.

18 Seth Dowland's book *Family Values and the Rise of the Christian Right* (Philadelphia: University of Pennsylvania Press, 2015) offers a good survey of relevant US history, concentrating on the period from the 1970s to the turn of the millennium.

19 The situation is much more readily blamed on technology than on the prevalence of monogamy as a default setting for all relationships, although without the latter it would largely disappear (or at least be radically altered). But that's not the point I'm trying to make right now.

20 One clear example of this is in Eva Illouz's book *Why Love Hurts: A Sociological Explanation* (Cambridge: Polity, 2012). More insights about the role of capitalism in shaping dating and romance can be found in Moira Weigel's book *Labor of Love: The Invention of Dating* (New York: Farrar, Straus & Giroux, 2016).

21 See, for example, chapter 1 of Irving Singer's book *The Nature of Love: Plato to Luther* (Cambridge, MA: MIT Press, 2009), or Dwayne Moore's article 'Reconciling appraisal love and bestowal love," *Dialogue: Canadian Philosophical Review* 57 (2018), pp. 67–92.

22 *Down Girl: The Logic of Misogyny* (New York: Oxford University Press, 2017).

23 Intriguingly, where the parents are happier, this doesn't appear to be coming at the *expense* of non-parents. Everyone just seems to be happier in these countries.

24 Analyses of relevant data can be found in Jennifer Glass et al., "Parenthood and happiness: effects of work-family reconciliation policies in 22 OECD countries," *American Journal of Sociology* 122 (2016), pp. 886–929.

25 See, for example, David Kessler's book *Finding Meaning: The Sixth Stage of Grief* (New York: Scribner, 2019).

26 I discuss the gendered history of "crimes of passion" and "provocation" defenses in chapter 5 of *What Love Is*.

27 I wrote about Millennial attitudes to gender for the *New Statesman* (23 September 2019). The article can be read at: www.newstatesman.com/politics/2019/09/millennials-are-fine-being-vague-about-gender-and-thats-no-bad-thing.

28 The full episode is available to download from: www.car riejenkins.net/podcast/2017/9/11/season-1-episode-2-love-stories.

29 Sartre's 1938 novel *Nausea* is a central text of existentialist thought.

30 Benjamin Hadden and Raymond Knee, "Finding meaning in us: the role of meaning in life in romantic relationships," *Journal of Positive Psychology* 13 (2018), pp. 226–39.